How to Perfect Your
SELLING
SKILLS

How to Perfect Your

SELLING SKILLS

PAT WEYMES

First published in 1990 by
Kogan Page Ltd,
120 Pentonville Rd, London N1 9JN

Typeset by DP Photosetting, Aylesbury, Bucks
Printed and bound in Great Britain by
Biddles Ltd, Guildford & Kings Lynn

British Library Cataloguing in Publication Data
Weymes, Patrick
  How to perfect your selling skills.
  1. Salesmanship
  I. Title
  658.8′5

  ISBN 0-7494-0065-X
  ISBN 0-7494-0064-1 *pbk*

For Cara

◀ CONTENTS ▶

◀ INTRODUCTION ▶

Selling is, and always will be, a vital part of the development and progress of mankind. More than any other profession, selling has the most significant influence on the survival of the world's economy.

Robert Louis Stevenson once said 'Everyone lives by selling something' and indeed the most sophisticated inventions are useless unless somebody can find a way to communicate these ideas to the customer. Consider, for example, what we would be missing if Edison's light bulb had not been sold to the commercial world!

Today's sales executive is as far removed from the original commercial traveller as the electronic calculator is from the abacus. While the basic principles of selling remain the same, the attitudes of buyers are constantly changing. Today's customer can choose his requirements from a number of companies – each promising to fulfil his needs. Whom he gives his order to will be greatly influenced by the attitude, skill and technique of the salespeople competing for his signature.

Yet only in recent years has selling been regarded and recognised as a professional career for which formal training is essential. Most induction training concentrates on product knowledge and sales technique. The programme in this book recognises these important skills but also places emphasis on two other critical areas – the personal development of the salesperson and a real understanding of the target of all our efforts – the buyer.

This book also deals with the vitally important skills of communication, human relations and personal motivation, areas so often overlooked in the development of the salesperson.

Today, selling is an exciting and challenging career where the rewards are directly related to the results obtained. The successful salesperson can, through dedication and hard work, achieve the enviable position of controlling the way he leads his life. This is the ultimate in personal freedom.

Successful selling depends not just on a good product, but on your ability to convince the customer it is *your* product he needs.

Selling is not about products or services, it is about what those products or services do for people. Unless you can communicate to the customer in a pleasant, persuasive manner how your product will solve his problem, you simply will not sell.

This programme is an action programme. It is designed to make you a more effective salesperson. If you merely read through the following pages, no doubt you will pick up a few ideas. However, it cannot be emphasised strongly enough that for this book to work for you, it is essential that you follow the action steps and implement the ideas in all your sales activity. Commit yourself to action and you will see it reflected in positive results.

◀ CHAPTER 1 ▶

MOTIVATION IN SELLING

Motivation

Motivation is the major reason for our success or failure in selling. Without it we rarely rise above the level of the mediocre salesperson.

When you are trying to influence or motivate others to accept your proposition, it is practically impossible to do so unless you are motivated yourself. Similarly, you can hardly hope to make others feel good if you don't feel good about yourself.

To motivate the customer you must first motivate *yourself*.

Motivated people motivate others by their very presence and in turn create positive working conditions, which makes hard work enjoyable.

Personal motivation begins in believing in yourself. If *you* don't, nobody else will. You are unique, there is absolutely nobody else in this world quite like you, and you owe it to yourself to be as successful as you want to be. Your determination and willpower and a positive mental attitude are all that are required.

Your ability to succeed in the business world is not hereditary. You must identify and develop the skills necessary to achieve success as a professional salesperson.

The Gestalt theory, which is supported by scientific researchers, claims that the average man or woman uses no more than 20% of their mental capacity. This being the case, 80% of our brain power remains dormant and the potential for personal development is enormous.

If you can accept this theory then you will also accept that, whatever you have achieved at this moment in life, you have done so operating on no more than 20% of your ability.

Ask yourself the following 10 questions and write down the answers in the space provided:

1. What major achievements have you had in the past year?

   _____

   _____

2. What promises did you make to yourself that you failed to act on?

   _____

   _____

3. What promotions have you had in the past two years?

   _____

   _____

4. What real improvements have you made in your living standards?

   _____

   _____

5. What are you doing today that you were doing two years ago?

   _____

   _____

6. What do you expect to be doing in five years?

   _____

   _____

7. How many friends or colleagues have overtaken you on the road to success?

   _____

   _____

8. Have you written goals for what you really want out of life?

_____

_____

9. Are you presently realising your full potential?

_____

_____

10. When are you finally going to do something about it?

_____

_____

The conditioning process

The reasons why most of us rarely maximise our capabilities are the many influences that dictate our mental development. For example: how many times in the past few years have you had your enthusiasm for an idea or project dampened by someone saying 'Let's be realistic about this'? People who claim to be realists are too often the so-called 'experts' of our society. They have all the reasons why something can't be done. For every solution they will find a problem.

From early childhood, we are all conditioned by the attitudes and influences of others. Our parents, marriage partners, TV, newspapers, friends, colleagues and managers have all influenced us to think in a certain way. Sadly, many of these influences have been negative, and have resulted in our becoming what other people have wanted us to be, not what _we_ wanted or could have been ourselves.

Some of these statements may seem familiar:

Sounds much too good to be true.
Take my word for it, it's not as simple as it seems.
You may as well dream here as in bed.
I'm beginning to worry about you.
You don't have the education.

From the time we are born we are told to conform. We are told whom to talk to, when to talk and whom we should or should not be associated with. The result is so often that we have the same fears, biases and attitudes as our parents. We are told 'You will never be the man your father was'. After a while we begin to believe it and refuse even to try.

Throughout our school years, the conditioning process continues. Most education encourages conformity and this halts any opportunity for creative or individual expression.

As we get older, out of misguided concern, the people closest to us impose mental limitations on us by exclaiming 'If it was that easy, how come someone else hasn't done it before now?' or 'It's not *what* you know, it's *who* you know'.

Criticism also plays a major role in impeding our development. Being told that we are stupid, shy, ugly or clumsy eventually begins to sink in and part of us begins to believe it.

When we make mistakes we are penalised, so we eventually do things 'the way they have always been done'. We realise at last that the penalties for trying and failing are usually greater than the penalties for doing nothing at all. So we conform, thinking to ourselves, 'I'll have a go next year'. But next year never comes. Or as Herbert Kaufmann put it, 'you are the one who used to boast that you would do your uttermost ... some day'.

Write three 'conditioning' statements that have prevented you from achieving a desirable goal.

1. _____

2. _____

3. _____

Recognise these statements for what they are – somebody else's opinions on what they believe to be your capabilities.

Habits and attitudes

Adopting a positive attitude is the first step towards improving all other personal skills.

The founder of Combined Insurances, Clement Stone, once said 'there is little difference between people: the little difference is attitude but the big difference is whether it is positive or negative.'

Attitudes are merely habits of the mind that can be changed. They are the influences of past associations and experiences. We develop these habits, then they develop us.

You are what you are because of your attitude and the thoughts that dominate your mind. You will become only what your mental attitude indicates. Keep on telling yourself that you can't do something and you will automatically impose a personal limitation. That psychological 'ceiling' will remain until your mental attitude changes. Attitudes and habits tend to go together: change one and you automatically change the other.

The importance of a positive mental attitude is well illustrated by Marvin Gregory's story in his book *Bits and Pieces*.

He tells of a young bride who followed her soldier husband to camp on the edge of the desert in California. The only home they could find was a shack near an Indian village; the weather was unbearably hot, windy and dusty, and the only neighbours were Indians who spoke no English. When her husband was sent into the desert on manoeuvres, the conditions and her loneliness finally became too great and she wrote to her mother saying she could bear it no longer. Her mother replied with these words:

> 'Two men looked out from prison bars
> One saw mud, the other saw stars'

Feeling ashamed of herself, she began to *look* for stars. She made friends with the Indians and became fascinated by their culture and way of life. She also began to study the desert flora and fauna and soon discovered that the desert was not a desolate wasteland, but a place with its own unique beauty. She later became an expert on the region and even wrote a book on it.

What had changed? Not the desert; not the Indians. Simply by changing her own attitude she had transformed a miserable experience into a highly rewarding one.

One of the biggest stumbling blocks to our progress is not the market, not the lack of opportunities or the present state of the world's economy – the stumbling block is ourselves.

	YES	NO
Are you good-humoured in the morning?	☐	☐
Do you offer encouraging words to others	☐	☐
Do you always speak well of others?	☐	☐
Do you try to see the positive points in people?	☐	☐

ACTION

Do you approach all situations with an open mind? ☐ ☐

Can you take instruction from someone younger than yourself? ☐ ☐

Would you do someone a good turn if you were going to be the only person to know about it? ☐ ☐

Are you a peacemaker? ☐ ☐

Are you good-natured about a decision that goes against you? ☐ ☐

Do people like to be associated with you? ☐ ☐

The power of the imagination

Our imagination plays a bigger part in our lives than most of us realise. We act, or fail to act, not because of our willpower, as many of us believe, but because of our imagination.

Many of us have believed that willpower alone has been the dominating factor in achieving our goals, but while it is a major influencing factor, it is a scientific fact that, if your imagination is in conflict with your willpower, the imagination will win every time. For example, if you 'will' yourself to be successful at something while at the same time 'imagining' that you will fail, it is impossible to succeed.

Emil Coué was famous for his amazing cures through the method of autosuggestion. Remember the phrase 'every day in every way I am getting better and better'. He believed that the imagination was the key to self-cure.

He also maintained that all the negative thoughts we have about ourselves could be compared with driving nails into a plank of wood. The only way to get rid of these negative thoughts is to keep on replacing them with positive ideas until all the negatives are eliminated.

Perhaps you have seen a hypnotist selecting assistants for a public performance. He will tell an audience of 200 or so to clasp their hands and imagine that they can't open them. No matter how hard they try or how much they 'will' their hands to open, a number of them cannot do so.

When 'convinced' that the hypnotist's words are true, a good hypnotic subject can do surprising things. The subject who is told that he is at the North Pole will not only shiver and appear to be cold but will also develop goose-pimples. In the same way many of us are 'hypnotised' into thinking that we are destined to be failures, so we behave appropriately.

According to the experts the wings of the queen bee are much too small to support the weight of the body in flight. They are convinced that it is physically impossible for the bee to fly. The only conclusion they can come to is that the bee has not been informed!

Dr Maxwell Maltz has spent many years researching the subconscious power. His book *Psychocybernetics* is presently hailed as a classic in its field and tells us that: 'The nervous system cannot tell the difference between an "imagined" and a "real" experience and the nervous system reacts appropriately to what we imagine to be true.'

There is plenty of hard factual evidence to support his suggestions. Hospital beds all over the world are filled with people whose only reason for being there is that they imagine they are seriously ill. People have died when they should have lived, while others have lived when they should have died.

Look up the word 'placebo' in a dictionary and you will find it defined as 'a sugar pill given to humour a patient'. Placebos, while having absolutely no healing ingredients whatsoever, have achieved miraculous cures for the most painful of ailments, stomach ulcers being just one of them.

In the business world the imagination has just as much influence. The most successful people are those who set out to prove that 'it *can* be done'. A profile of some of the most successful business people in the world revealed one common denominator – none of them ever imagines, or entertains the thought of, failure in any undertaking.

Success or the lack of it depends greatly on your imagination and what you tell yourself. Researchers into human behaviour have concluded that people will get only what their mental attitude indicates – in other words, if you think negatively the result will be negative, whereas if you think positively you will create an atmosphere which makes positive results a certainty. An unknown writer put it very well when he wrote:

> If you think you are beaten, you are,
> If you think you dare not, you don't,
> If you'd like to win, but think you can't,
> It's almost certain you won't.
> Life's battles don't always go

Willpower, consciously and consistently applied, is the key to overcoming potential obstacles.

To the stronger or faster man:
But sooner or later, the man who wins
Is the man who thinks he can.

Some questions for you to consider:

A. How would you feel on Monday morning, if you thought it was Tuesday?

B. What level of sales would you achieve if nobody had told you what your sales target is?

C. How much are you influenced by what other people claim they 'can' or 'cannot' do?

D. List five things that you have always told yourself that you 'cannot' do. Indicate whether these were physical restrictions or mental ones imposed by your imagination.

1. _____ Physical/Mental

2. _____ Physical/Mental

3. _____ Physical/Mental

4. _____ Physical/Mental

5. _____ Physical/Mental

E. Instead of saying 'That is the way I am,' start saying 'That is the way I used to be but today is another story.'

Goal-setting

Having talked about the conditioning process and the influence of our imagination, we realise that what we are now is a direct result of the influences and experiences of our past. It must follow then, that what we do today will shape our future.

You have a choice to make – right now. You can be a passive bystander in life, hoping that success will embrace you. You can wistfully daydream your life away or you can determine the shape of your future by planning and setting definite goals. You have the ability to achieve what you want. Whether you enforce that ability with desire, energy and motivation to reach your objective is your decision alone. Setting and achieving your personal goals lead to freedom and the ultimate luxury of choosing how you live your life.

Set realistic goals

Your goals must be realistic. They should present a challenge but still be possible to attain. If you want to be President of the United States of America, you must first be an American citizen. So, unless you were born in the USA or are a naturalised American, setting that goal would be pointless.

Your future is dictated by the goals you set today.

It is absolutely imperative that your goals are your own and are not unfairly influenced by others. It is, after all, your life, and sacrificing your desires for the sake of others will impact your motivation in a negative way.

Next, you must really want whatever goals you decide on. Anything worthwhile usually involves hard work and goal-setting is no exception. You will need all your energy and motivation if things do not go according to plan. Developing the ability to picture vividly in your mind what it is you want will help you to achieve the end result.

Having decided on the goal, analyse exactly what you have to do to achieve it.

Anticipate the obstacles that you will inevitably have to overcome and, of course, what you're going to do to solve them.

There must be start and finish dates. A football match without a time limit would be pointless and there would be no winner.

The rewards to you on achievement are extremely important. List them in as much detail as possible. They will feed your motivation and urge you on to success.

Your goals will obviously span different areas of your life – your career, your family life, your own development.

An airline pilot would never attempt to fly a plane without a flight plan. He may have flown the same route for years, but he would never trust his memory. You too must have a written plan. Writing down your goals helps to clarify your thinking and strengthens the commitment you are making with yourself. Fuzzy, misty thoughts will produce fuzzy, misty results. On the other hand, an organised plan will spur you into action and increase your determination to succeed.

It is part of our nature as human beings to strive towards some desirable goal. If we have nothing to aim for, we become bored and frustrated. Life doesn't seem worthwhile. Take charge of your life. Replace the frustration with some action planning and spend your time and energy in making your life better for you and your family.

Allow your goals to be flexible. You will be a different person in five years' time and what you now think will make you happy may change in that time. It is also a human trait to fast become dissatisfied with what we have achieved and begin searching for something else. Goal-setting should therefore be interpreted as a flexible instrument to help us move from where we are now to where we want to be. While it is difficult to predict exactly what you will be like in 10 years' time, you can at least dictate the direction in which you want to move.

It does work. If you believe you can achieve your goal, if you sincerely want it, and you work single-mindedly to get it, you will be successful.

List all the goals you would like to achieve in your life, no matter how outrageous they may appear right now. You should consider every area of your development such as:

Career goals – positions you would like to achieve; how you would like to develop within your company; where you would like to see yourself in two, three and five years. . . .

1. _____ 6. _____

2. _____ 7. _____

3. _____ 8. _____

4. _____ 9. _____

5. _____ 10. _____

Personal goals – write down everything you have ever wanted to achieve – the places that you would like to visit and everything you have always wanted out of life.

1. _____ 6. _____

2. _____ 7. _____

3. _____ 8. _____

4. _____ 9. _____

5. _____ 10. _____

Domestic and family goals – what you would like to achieve for your family; what the family would like to do together (improved relationships, going on holidays as a unit, etc.); plans for putting children through college. . . .

1. ———————— 6. ————————

2. ———————— 7. ————————

3. ———————— 8. ————————

4. ———————— 9. ————————

5. ———————— 10. ————————

Educational goals – your further development; courses you would like to attend; qualifications you would like to attain. . . .

1. ———————— 6. ————————

2. ———————— 7. ————————

3. ———————— 8. ————————

4. ———————— 9. ————————

5. ———————— 10. ————————

(Repeat this exercise for material, recreational, spiritual and physical goals or any other area of development that appears to be relevant.)

Prioritise the goals

List, in order of priority, the 10 goals that you consider to be the most important at this stage of your life:

1. ———————— 6. ————————

2. ———————— 7. ————————

3. ———————— 8. ————————

4. ———————— 9. ————————

5. ———————— 10. ————————

Transfer each of these goals to a goal-setting chart like the one following and, using the recommended formula, make a determined effort to follow them through to completion. Once you are convinced that the formula works apply it to all future goal-setting.

Goal to be achieved _____

Action steps required to achieve goal

1. _____   6. _____
2. _____   7. _____
3. _____   8. _____
4. _____   9. _____
5. _____   10. _____

Obstacles or difficulties to be eliminated on the way

1. _____
2. _____
3. _____

Start date ___ / ___ / ___   Finish date ___ / ___ / ___

Reward to me on achievement of goal

1. _____   11. _____
2. _____   12. _____
3. _____   13. _____
4. _____   14. _____
5. _____   15. _____
6. _____   16. _____
7. _____   17. _____
8. _____   18. _____
9. _____   19. _____
10. _____   20. _____

Procrastination

Procrastination has been called the 'thief of time', the 'effectiveness killer', and we all fall into the trap of inaction at some time or another. The first step to banishing this destructive trait forever is to recognise the futility of it and resolve to be ruthless in its elimination.

Procrastination solves nothing, but the consequences, particularly for a salesperson, can be devastating. It leads to frustration, anxiety and a host of unsolved problems that generally only get worse.

Why do we do it? The most common reasons are:

1. *To avoid doing something unpleasant.* Sadly, ignoring unpleasant tasks or problems will not make them disappear. If you put off going to a dentist with a toothache, one day you will lose the tooth. The best approach is to weight up the benefits of action *now* as opposed to the results of further delay. Usually this will provide the necessary incentive to get going.

2. *Lack of confidence.* This can be very damaging. Put something off for long enough and the problem will seem impossible to solve. Break the task into small, manageable steps and each small success will feed your self-confidence and urge further action.

3. *Fear of rejection or failure.* This is a very human emotion and one that may be described as an occupational hazard. Every salesperson has suffered from this. Let's face it, few customers are actually going to rush out of their offices and welcome us as long-lost relatives. They will be very cautious about spending money and may seem rude and aggressive at times. Remember, if we avoid failure or rejection, we will almost certainly avoid success as well. Only through making mistakes can we learn and mature.

4. *Bad habits.* In our profession this is a very common problem. Many salespeople will put off writing quotations, making call-backs or checking out customer queries, with the result that orders, and tempers, are lost. This is merely habit. Resolve with determination to change and you will find that you complete tasks with much less effort than before.

It is worthwhile keeping in mind the following quotation:

> 'If you want to make an easy job seem hard, just
> keep putting off doing it.'

The motivation to be gained from completing long overdue tasks can be considerable. To prove this point to yourself list three tasks that you have been putting off, set a short-term timetable for their completion and start now!

1. _____ To be completed by ___ / ___ / ___

2. _____ To be completed by ___ / ___ / ___

3. _____ To be completed by ___ / ___ / ___

Developing a selling personality

If you can accept the influence of your imagination over your behaviour, then you must also accept that it is possible to change or develop your personality for the better.

Personality is not like a round face or blue eyes. We can do little about our physical characteristics. We can, however, through a positive attitude and determination do something about our personality, because personality or the lack of it is merely an attitude of the mind.

It was Abraham Lincoln who said 'People are only as happy as they allow themselves to be.' That statement is also true of personality. How much or how little we achieve in life is governed very much by what we tell ourselves. Believe that you are shy, aggressive, easygoing or anxious and your behaviour will tend to support your own concept of who you are.

It is essential in selling to appraise your strengths and weaknesses constantly. The successful sales personality will have a combination of the qualities summed up in the phrase PERSONAL SUCCESS SKILLS. When considering these qualities, bear in mind that every single one of them can be acquired.

P – Perseverance. The ability to continue on your course of action despite difficulties or opposition. In selling, the efforts expended today are rarely reflected in today's results. We may have to call many times before we finally reap the rewards. We must keep uppermost in our minds that in our profession the only alternative to perseverance is failure to sell.

E – Empathy. Probably the most important attribute in selling: the ability to put yourself mentally in the other person's shoes. It is the skill of experiencing the other person's feelings and emotions imaginatively.

Many people confuse empathy with sympathy, yet there is a distinct difference. Sympathy literally means to 'be in favour of or agreement with one's mood or opinions', whereas empathy means to really understand, but not necessarily to agree.

Empathy only becomes possible if you can mentally see the selling process from the buyer's point of view. There is an old Spanish expression: 'In order to be a bullfighter you must first learn to be a bull'. In order to be a successful salesperson you must first learn to be a customer.

R – Resilience. The ability to bounce back from disappointment and recover strength quickly. In the role of a salesperson, there will be many times when you get that 'Maybe I'm not cut out to be a salesperson' feeling. Just about every professional has uttered those words at some time or another.

We need resilience to remind us that we are members of one of the most exciting and most frustrating professions in the world, and that every every day will bring new opportunities and many disappointments. How much time we spend recovering from disappointments will dictate the opportunities we take advantage of.

Thomas Edison suffered hundreds of failures before he finally invented the light bulb. In fact many of the greatest inventions of our time would still be mere laboratory toys were it not for the resilience of their creators.

S – Sincerity. Being genuine and honest without conceit or pretence – one of those qualities that is rarely faked with any success. Your customer must know that you mean what you say, and that you pass on only correct information.

O – Open mind. An absence of prejudiced or narrow-minded views. It means allowing mental access to the opinions and views of others in an effort to learn from their experiences.

N – Neat appearance. If you claim to work for a successful company with superior products, then you must dress in a manner that is consistent with your company's image. You would be reluctant to buy goods that are badly wrapped out of concern for the contents. Similarly, the customer will be reluctant to buy from you if you are untidy or slovenly in appearance.

A - Ambition to succeed. The burning desire to achieve your predetermined objectives. The only place where success comes before work is in the dictionary, and so ambition must be coupled with an active determination to achieve your personal and business goals.

L - Loyalty. Being totally faithful to people you are under an obligation to defend or support. Customers find it refreshing to hear a salesperson speak well of his company and colleagues.

S - Self-confidence. Our personal belief in our own abilities. The only way we can develop our self-confidence is through the experience of making mistakes and scoring little victories. It is easier to have faith in yourself if you can see your success.

Confidence or the lack of it is an attitude of mind. If you tell yourself subconsciously that you can't do something, you will find in every case that you were right. 'Skill and confidence', as an old proverb puts it, 'are an unconquered army'.

If confidence comes from belief, then logically it follows that the only way we can develop that belief is through action. Take the example of a baby taking his first steps. He will wobble and fall many times but in his determation to walk he will dismiss completely all the failed attempts. It was Confucius who said that failure is not falling down: it is falling down and refusing to get back up again.

U - Understanding of human relations. The human touch – showing kindness and consideration to other people. In selling terms this means practising and developing a combination of the various skills that will be discussed in a separate section, The Skills of Human Relations (p. 48 below).

C - Common sense. The mental ability to absorb facts and learn from a new experience. All successful salespeople must be alert to opportunities to improve their performance. They aren't satisfied with today's results, they want to do better tomorrow. It also means being able to focus your strengths and efforts on the task in hand.

C - Cooperation. Working together with your colleagues, subordinates and superiors as a team trying to achieve one common goal. Putting aside petty differences of opinion for the sake of the company objectives. Working with your customers and making conscious efforts to offer a complete and flexible service.

E – Enthusiasm. The magic spark that gets support without ever having to ask for it. Not only is it contagious, it is also the greatest motivator known to man. It is the burning inner drive that helps us to persude people without pressurising them. It was Emerson who said that without enthusiasm nothing great was ever achieved.

We develop enthusiasm in selling from three main areas. Firstly, we must develop a belief in ourselves and in our ability to do the job. Secondly, we must have total conviction in our product and a sincere belief that the customer will receive genuine benefit from his purchase. Thirdly, we must have a sincere belief in the integrity of our company and colleagues.

The salesperson who truly believes in each of these areas will automatically feel enthusiastic. In no other field of endeavour is there such a wide scope of opportunity for those enthusiastic enough to meet the challenge.

Always keep one point uppermost in your mind: the prospective buyer will never think any more highly of your product than you do.

S – Simplicity. Speaking a language that others understand. All the skills and sales techniques are useless unless you have the ability to communicate thoughts and ideas to others in a manner that is acceptable and easily understood.

S – Self-motivation. Literally means 'inspiration to action'. There are two types of motivation. *External* motivation operates through fear or incentive imposed by external influences, such as, for example, a sales manager. This type of motivation is short-term and ceases once the need or fear has been satisfied or eliminated.

The second type of motivation, *internal* motivation, is the more powerful because it is long-term and alters inbred attitudes. It comes from developing a sincere desire for the things you want most out of your job, your career, or your life. As an example: it has often been said that you can bring a horse to the well but you can't make him drink; however, you will have no trouble getting him to drink if you begin by making him thirsty!

S – Sense of direction. A salesperson without a daily plan and daily targets is like a car without a steering wheel. Be crystal-clear about what you want and keep the benefits of your goals at the front of your mind all the time.

K – Knowledge. Constantly searching for more information about the marketplace and the trends of future months and years. Striving to perfect and update selling techniques, to improve sales presentations and to increase orders.

I – Integrity. Honourable standards of ethics and professionalism. Our profession operates to a set of accepted principles that must guide our conduct. By the very nature of our job we are exposed to temptations daily. Exercising a high standard of integrity will, at the very least, establish your credibility as a professional.

L – Listening ability. Making a conscious effort to hear. A winner listens, a loser just waits until it's his turn to talk. Joe Girard the Detroit salesman who is credited in the Guinness Book of Records as 'the world's greatest salesman' put it in a nutshell when he said 'God gave us two ears and one tongue so we could listen more than we talk'. It was that philosophy that helped him sell 1,425 individual new cars in one year.

L – Leadership skills. The ability to influence or direct your own course of action through your own efforts. We are either the masters or the victims of our destiny. Every salesperson has the option of being the passenger or the driver in his career.

S – Sense of humour. The ability to appreciate or expess amusement. Selling is a very serious business but we need to have the ability to introduce humour and the common sense to use it where appropriate.

If you go back, you will see that what you have just completed are the keys to PERSONAL SUCCESS SKILLS.

As a guide to your self-analysis, fill in this Sales Personality Development graph. Seek the unbiased opinion of two other people when filling it in. What you may discover is that their view of you is quite different from the picture you have of yourself.

PERSONALITY DEVELOPMENT GRAPH

	0	1	2	3	4	5	6	7	8	9	10
PERSEVERANCE											
EMPATHY											
RESILIENCE											
SINCERITY											
OPEN MIND											
NEAT APPEARANCE											
AMBITION TO SUCCEED											
LOYALTY											
SELF-CONFIDENCE											
UNDERSTANDING OF HUMAN RELATIONS											
COMMON SENSE											
COOPERATION											
ENTHUSIASM											
SIMPLICITY											
SELF-MOTIVATION											
SENSE OF DIRECTION											
KNOWLEDGE											
INTEGRITY											
LISTENING ABILITY											
LEADERSHIP SKILLS											
SENSE OF HUMOUR											
	0	1	2	3	4	5	6	7	8	9	10

◄ CHAPTER 2 ►

COMMUNICATION SKILLS

Communication

There are many definitions of the word 'communication'. The most comprehensive is 'the interchange of thoughts, opinions, ideas, or information by speech, writing or signs'. Communication is also an exchange of feelings and attitudes. If there is no agreement on these ideas, conflict may occur.

It is impossible to communicate effectively if you:

- neglect to listen to what the other person is saying;
- stubbornly refuse to see another point of view;
- refuse to accept that others are entitled to their views and opinions;
- over-react to others' comments and views.

It isn't necessary to agree, but there must be recognition that the needs of others are as legitimate as your own.

The professional salesperson has the ability to convey ideas to others. This is an essential quality. Powerful and stimulating ideas are lost unless a way is found to communicate them to customers.

Transmitting the message

Good ideas must be enhanced by effective communication.

Even if you are the perfect communicator, you still have to deal with the rest of us. Bear in mind that we speak at the rate of 150 to 200 words per minutes, yet our listener is capable of grasping ideas at 10 times that rate.

We must recognise the importance of keeping our message interesting in order to hold the listener's attention.

At least four messages are present in every message we send:

- what we mean to say;
- what we actually say;
- what the other person hears;
- what the other person thinks he hears.

How many times have you heard people say 'that's not what I meant to say', or 'that may be what you tried to say but that is not what I heard'? Difficulty in expressing our thoughts is an international problem. An Australian motor insurance company received the following explanations from policy holders:

'The pedestrian had no idea which way to go. So I ran over him.'
'An invisible car came out of nowhere, struck my vehicle and vanished.'

It seems even experienced newspaper editors cannot escape:

'Passengers Hit by Cancelled Trains'
'Man Denies Committing Suicide'

Some barriers to effective communication in selling

Your audience is constantly bombarded with competing sights, sounds, thoughts and ideas; it is essential to be conscious of the sales communication barriers. Some of the most common are as follows:

Exaggeration
It is important in your enthusiasm not to oversell the benefits of your products. The use of superlatives should be avoided. Claiming that your product or service is 'the finest', 'the biggest', or 'the best' is likely to be disbelieved by the customer. It is a far better idea to talk in more moderate terms about your product.

Vagueness and generalities
It is easy to fall into the trap of using statements like 'Everybody says we give the best service', 'Most companies have found', or 'It is generally

accepted by people in the field'. Who are these people and on what facts were their statements based? It is acceptable to use these statements *provided* they are backed up by the expert's name, the relevant knowledge and the facts.

Egocentric language

Certain expressions discourage a customer from buying, so avoid saying things like 'If I were you', or 'If you want my opinion', 'Think about what I said' and 'My advice would be'. Any of these could create a negative selling environment. Changing 'I think' to 'Don't *you* think?' can help make a sale.

Jaw-breakers

Customers are not impressed when they hear a salesperson using big words. Mark Twain once said 'I never write "metropolis" when I get paid the same money for writing "city".'

Confusing facts with opinions

A man who lost £60,000 in a business deal was convinced that he was ruined because he had lost that amount of money. It was a fact that he had lost £60,000, but it was only his opinion that he was ruined. Once he realised this, he was able to recover and go on to become more successful than ever before.

We are very much influenced by the opinions of other people, again reacting to them as if they too were facts.

Among the barriers to effective communication are the personality, education, status, background, religion, age and emotional state of the sender or the receiver. Each will play a major role in the communication process.

Words

Words will not always have the same meaning to other people as they have to you. In fact there are over 14,000 dictionary definitions of the 500 most commonly used words in the English language. It is not hard to see why communication is so difficult. Remember, a useful guideline to communication in selling is that anything capable of misinterpretation *will* be misinterpreted. The following story illustrates:

During the First World War the following message was radioed from one camp to another: 'The Germans are advancing on west flanks. Send reinforcements.' When it was received at its final destination it read: 'The Germans are dancing on wet planks. Send three and fourpence.'

Effective listening skills

Most of this chapter has been concerned with the sending side of communication; however, it is essential to realise that listening is equally important. Without effective listening there can be no effective communication.

We learn by listening. How would you feel about a doctor who wouldn't listen to your complaint or about a barrister who didn't ask you any questions? Good listening skills are vital to the sales profession. Make a definite point of developing the following listening habits:

When the customer is talking, say absolutely nothing.

Let the customer know that he has your total, undivided attention. Maintain eye contact. If you find looking into a customer's eyes intimidating, look at the top of his nose – he won't know the difference. It is recommended that eye contact should be maintained between 65% and 80% of the time.

Watch your body language. Show the customer that his comments are of interest. Respond physically by moving forward or nodding your head in agreement.

Listen for signals. Try to concentrate on the meaning of the message and what is being said, not on the person or the manner in which it is being said.

Don't get emotionally involved. If the customer makes a critical comment about you or your company, listen carefully or you may miss a key point. Encourage your customers to bring their complaints to you, not to your competitors.

Communicate your understanding by using expressions like 'I see' and 'I understand'.

Communication is a two-way process – without effective listening there can be no effective communication.

35

Personal space

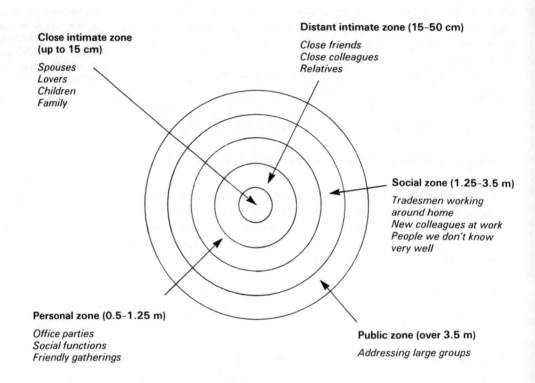

Close intimate zone (up to 15 cm)

Spouses
Lovers
Children
Family

Distant intimate zone (15–50 cm)

Close friends
Close colleagues
Relatives

Social zone (1.25–3.5 m)

Tradesmen working around home
New colleagues at work
People we don't know very well

Personal zone (0.5–1.25 m)

Office parties
Social functions
Friendly gatherings

Public zone (over 3.5 m)

Addressing large groups

Communication wavelengths

An important aspect of our ability to communicate is talking and listening on the same 'wavelength'. People often feel most uncomfortable when meeting others for the first time and a conversation is forced on them by the circumstances. Understanding these wavelengths assists better communication. Many writers on the subject indicate that there are five levels of communication:

Level 5: Cliché conversation

Practically all greetings are followed up with, 'How are you?', 'Been on holiday?', 'Nice day' and so on. As we can't talk to people in clichés all day we will either terminate the conversation and move on or we will move into the next level. It is this level that involves the greatest number of people.

Level 4: Small talk

This includes neutral topics such as the weather or TV programmes or observations about our surroundings. It is unlikely either party will have any conflict at this level. This involves about half as many people as the cliché level.

Level 3: Facts and opinions

Salespeople should make an effort to get to this level as quickly as possible, as this is where selling should take place. It involves the exchange of ideas, facts and opinions. Communication is more comfortable at this level and involves a certain amount of risk because opinions are expressed.

Level 2: Emotions and feelings

For this level to be achieved, there must be an atmosphere of mutual trust and respect. It is generally reserved for a select number of friends and colleagues and members of your family. As it involves the emotions, people may open their hearts to you and it should be interpreted as a vote of confidence in your friendship. In a selling situation, while it is acceptable to express your 'feelings', beware of embarrassing the buyer by becoming emotional.

Level 1: Peak communication

Reserved only for the most intimate of friends, lovers and marital partners. Requires the highest levels of trust between both parties, and the circle of people communicated with at this level will be few. This level can also be communicated through body language such as touching, smiling or looking.

For a salesperson, it is obvious that selling can take place comfortably only at level 3. However, levels 5 and 4 must be acknowledged on the way to achieving a proper selling level. It is easy to understand how difficult communication is if the other person is responding in clichés and vice versa. It is hardly correct to describe such exchanges as communication.

From what you have just read, identify these levels of communication:

'Mr Smith, what would you say if I told you that, based on our previous discussion, my company can save you £50,000 per year?'   Level ____

'I felt let down and hurt by what you said to me, particularly when we have had such a good close relationship in the past.'   Level ____

'I see that the company next door are expanding. It really does not surprise me, they employ very good people.'   Level ____

Body language

The importance of body language should never be underestimated. Actions do speak louder than words. The ability to observe and understand the nonverbal messages we send or receive is an important skill in selling.

Close to 90% of a message is transmitted nonverbally. This is why face-to-face communication is more effective than telephone conversations. Some salespeople prefer to deliver their quotations in person. They watch the eyes and posture of their customer and adjust their negotiation according to carefully observed reactions.

The reason why we should learn to read body language is that, when it is in conflict with the spoken word, the body language is nearly always the correct portrayal of the truth.

While it is only in recent years that people have really become aware of the importance of reading body language, much explanatory work has already been done by authorities like Desmond Morris and Julius Fast. Salespeople should take time to learn body signals and apply them in selling situations.

Understanding body language is a vital selling tool.

One chapter is not sufficient to cover this entire subject, but there are some excellent books available on it. I propose to outline some of the areas of body language applicable to professional salespersons.

Personal space

Everybody has his own personal space and others invade it at their peril. If you were to look at a photograph of yourself with a group of close friends and compare it with the distance you keep from the handyman, you can see immediately the importance of keeping your distance when you are approaching a customer for the first time.

Intruding on another's personal zone may cause such physiological changes to take place within his body that he will become agitated and want to move to a safer distance, even though he may smile and pretend to enjoy it.

1. Intimate distance (up to 50 cm)
People guard this distance as if it were their own personal property. We see it every day on trains and buses, where people sit in the middle of the seat, or put a bag beside them, discouraging others from sitting too close. The close intimate distance (up to 15 cm) indicates people who are allowed to touch, such as marriage partners, lovers or children. The far intimate distance (15–50 cm) is reserved for close friends. As the intimacy of the relationship decreases, the distance increases.

2. Close personal zone (0.5–1.25 m)
This is the distance at which we stand from others at a party, social events and friendly gatherings.

3. Social zone (1.25–3.5 m)
This is the distance one allows when communication is inevitable with strangers such as the washing-machine repair man or a new colleague at work. Most selling is done at this distance because this permits a certain amount of protection. The close social zone (1.25 m) should be observed when discussing business with the receptionist. Standing too close may inhibit the receptionist from continuing to work.

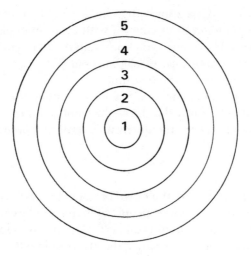

Level 5: Cliché conversation
Level 4: Small talk
Level 3: Facts and opinions
Level 2: Emotions and feelings
Level 1: Peak communication

Personal space

4. Public zone (over 3.5 m)

Reserved for addressing a large group of people, as at a social function or lecture.

People who live in cities have different attitudes to personal space than people born and brought up on farms. If you spend all your working days in buses, trains and lifts, in close contact with others, you will feel differently about a stranger standing a metre away than a farmer would. People's sensitivity to space has to be acknowledged and observed. So keep your distance.

Allow the customer to remain comfortable by learning the rules of personal space.

Body contact

It is perfectly acceptable for a manager to clap a subordinate on the back after a job well done. What would happen if the situation was reversed? A salesperson would need to have a good relationship with a customer to be able to touch the customer because to do so would mean invading his personal space. Putting your arm around a customer's shoulder may communicate a closeness perceived by the salesperson, but rejected by the customer.

I know of one salesperson who lost a sale because he touched the customer's lapel and said 'nice suit'.

When people shake hands many things are communicated. The weak handshake suggests a weak character and (while we know it is untrue) the other person may feel he can dominate you. The weak handshake might imply you are not pleased to meet the other person, while a 'bonecrusher' might imply you wish to dominate or are seeking to impress.

One thing many salespeople have been associated with are excessively strong handshakes. Regrettably, it does not communicate the image of a helpful salesperson.

Handshakes should be warm and strong without being 'wet fish' or knuckle grinding. Sometimes customers will give a limp handshake, but don't read too much into it. They may have other issues on their mind and be unaware of the type of welcome they are conveying.

Hand-to-face gestures

Any spontaneous movement of the hand to the face is an indication that the person is uncomfortable and probably lying. These gestures are a relic from our childhood days. A child who doesn't want to hear that it is time for bed will cover her ears. If there is something frightening on

TV she will cover her eyes with her arms. If she tells a lie her hand will immediately go to her mouth in an attempt to conceal the untruthful words. As we get older, we learn to refine our reactions, but the basic attempt to conceal the lie continues.

If, when you ask a customer 'What are my chances of getting the order?' the reply ('I'd say they are pretty good') is accompanied by pulling the collar, scratching the neck, rubbing the ear or the eye, pretending to scratch the nose or covering the mouth, the implication is that the person is lying. Why would a person who is sitting comfortably suddenly respond with these gestures? Rephrase the question when the person is comfortable and see if you get the same reaction. If you do, change your approach: the person is not sold.

Arm-folding

A husband arrives home late for dinner (again). His wife is standing in the kitchen with her arms folded – indicating a row is brewing. Each movement of the body has its own expressive function, whether conscious or unconscious. If people have negative thoughts about you or your product they may fold their arms as a 'shield' against your unfavourable message. This standard gesture is seen at union/management meetings where people are among strangers or are seen as rivals.

In a one-to-one conversation, if the other person folds his arms in the middle of your conversation it may mean that he disagrees, even though the facial expression and the spoken word imply otherwise. Persisting in this line of discussion may prove fruitless.

If the folded arm is accompanied by clenched fists it suggests that the person may explode at any moment.

Interesting research has been carried out on the folded-arms position. The tests indicated that, when the listener folds his arms, not only is he paying less attention but he is likely to have more critical comments to make about the speaker.

Tests carried out on two groups of students corroborated these findings. Alan Pease in his excellent book on the subject, *Signals* (Bantam Books) tells us that:

> One group was asked to attend a series of talks and instructed to take up a relaxed sitting position with legs and arms uncrossed. A second group was instructed to keep their arms crossed firmly against their chests. The results showed the group who had their arms folded learned and remembered 38% less than the group who had their arms

unfolded. The second group had more negative thoughts about the speaker and the lectures.

Some people claim that arm folding is a comfortable way to sit, and this is a legitimate argument when the chair has no arms or there is no table on which to lean. If this situation does not prevail the person is probably negative and the sales approach should be altered accordingly.

Eye contact

Some nonverbal signals seem to be beyond any conscious control. One of these is eye pupil dilation. You may force yourself to look at a person's face while talking, thereby pretending to have an interest you don't feel, but you cannot consciously control the size of your eye pupils.

The pupils will change size with the interest an individual feels. For example, if a man is looking at a woman and feels attracted to her, his pupils will dilate. Women react the same way to men. If a poker player has an exciting hand his pupils will dilate also. Similarly, if a customer is offered an interesting proposal his eye pupils will automatically enlarge.

Looking into a customer's eyes at the precise moment the price is mentioned will reveal the customer's surprise at the price being lower than expected, shock that it is so high, or a totally neutral reaction. It may happen that the buyer expresses shock verbally on hearing the price, only to be betrayed by lack of pupil reaction. That is one reason why quotations should be delivered personally, because the real reaction to price can be gauged. As people's mood changes from positive to negative the eye pupil will contract or dilate accordingly. When a person becomes excited the pupils may dilate up to four times their normal size. On the other hand when a person is in an angry or negative mood the pupils will contract to half their normal size.

When we are listening, our eye contact is as high as 100%, but when we are talking our eye contact can be as low as zero, and that doesn't help our skill in communicating. Beware of staring, ogling or running your eyes up and down another person. It makes others feel most uncomfortable.

Facial expressions

Facial expressions are the most obvious forms of nonverbal communication. A salesperson, however, should read the facial expression in relation to other body movements, which are much more reliable indicators of real feelings because they are more difficult to control.

Body posture
Body language is hard to fake at any time and posture is no different. An exception to the rule may occur on the beach, where a man passing an attractive woman may consciously pull in his stomach to give a more virile appearance.

Observing the customer's posture is obviously important, particularly if he sits up in the middle of a particular point, signifying interest. Slouching in the chair indicates a lack of enthusiasm for the point under discussion.

It is believed that the body gives up to 80,000 different signals, all significantly meaningful. Taking the time to learn some of them is an important part of a salesperson's acquisition of subtle skills.

In the same way, it is important to be alert to your own and to other people's body language. How we say things is often more important than the message itself.

The use of videotape and audio equipment has made it possible to capture and analyse human behaviour. Often these signals are so minute that they can be seen only by studying a videotape frame by frame.

Body language is a fascinating area of study to which many people are devoting their time. By observing more, by improving your powers of perception and by knowing as much as possible about your customers, you should be able to translate more accurately your own non-verbal messages and those of others.

To improve your ability to read body language follow these recommended steps:

1. Take 15 minutes every day to read others' body language.

2. Look for inconsistencies between what people are saying and what their body language indicates.

3. When you are watching TV turn the volume down and see if you can follow the storyline by observing the body language. After a short time turn up the volume and see if you were correct!

4. Never miss an opportunity to observe others' body language, at

airports, parties or social gatherings. Every human emotion is expressed nonverbally at these places.

10 ways to better communication

1. Use vocal variety
Try to develop the characteristics of a good speaking voice so that people will want to listen. Appealing articulation:

is *pleasant* in tone, conveying warmth;
is *natural* for the sake of sincerity;
has *enthusiasm* to strengthen advocacy of a point;
contains *vocal variety* to avoid monotony;
has *volume and clarity* so that the information is easily assimilated.

2. Make it persuasive
In order for people to change views or firmly held beliefs, three things must happen. First, they need a rational appeal to logically justify this new belief. Second, they must become motivated emotionally. Third, they must have sincere belief in the source of the information. The Greek philosopher Aristotle referred to them as the three indispensable pillars of persuasion.

1. Fact – the information must be logical and truthful.
2. Emotion – to draw people to your cause their emotions must be aroused.
3. Credibility – to persuade, you must be manifestly knowledgeable, authoritative and of the highest integrity.

3. Present your ideas in an orderly manner
The difference between a box of coloured glass and a stained glass window is organisation. Relate your points in a logical pattern so that others can follow it easily.

4. Use 'you' appeal
Phrase your articulation to highlight the interest of the listener. Where possible use 'you' rather than 'I'. Ideas that are of no 'personal' interest to the listener will fall on deaf ears.

5. Use the KISS method
Avoid eclipsing the main point of your message by overcommunicating.

KISS means: 'Keep It Short and Sweet' or, as others would prefer: 'Keep it Simple, Stupid'.

6. Be stimulating

A question I often put to delegates on courses is this: 'If you were trying to turn on members of the opposite sex, what part of their anatomy would you concentrate on?' I will leave it to your imagination rather than mention some of the many responses offered by the delegate.

Surprisingly enough, few, if any, ever give the correct response: it is of course 'the brain'. If you can find a way to stimulate the other person's brain you are in business. Good selling is based on this very principle. Stimulate others by getting them to use their brain: by asking questions, showing interest in their interests, asking for their advice or opinions and making them feel important. It really works!

7. Be conscious of bias

Many of us have preconceived notions about different groups of people – for example, 'when you've met one salesman you've met them all'. Avoid stereotyping, labelling or generalising about any person or group. We are all individuals with unique beliefs, attitudes, feelings and emotions.

Similarly, the reverse is also true. The labels that people put on *you* can have quite an impact on how they perceive your message. Consider the implications of your comments on the receiver and have regard for his feelings.

How do you discover you are biased? Test yourself frequently. Assume that you are in a restaurant with a friend – somebody of whom you are particularly fond. By accident, that person spills red wine over your best clothes. How would you respond? Now the same situation but change the close friend to someone you don't like. Again the red wine is spilt over you. How would you respond now? If your reaction is different, then you are biased.

8. Be a mirror of your message

If you decide to give a talk on personal appearance, obviously it is important that you own attire is above criticism. A father is unlikely to achieve success if he lectures his children on the effects of smoking while he has a cigarette in his hand. A salesperson claiming to work for a successful company must project a successful image in manner, attire and presentation.

9. Watch body language

Set aside a period of time every day to study the body language of others. At the same time be conscious of your own body talk. When you are talking to people watch out for spontaneous physical reaction and try to work out what signal is coming across. Observe gestures, posture and expressions and check to see if the signals are consistent with what is being said or contrary to it.

10. Empathise all the time

Only with empathy can you recognise the needs that others have. This helps to tailor the message in a manner that promises to fulfil their needs. Consider the listeners' feelings and help them to relax by speaking courteously and sincerely.

◀ CHAPTER 3 ▶

THE HUMAN SIDE OF BUYING AND SELLING

Human relations

In today's business world professional selling techniques can never be comprehensive without practising the skills of human relations.

Without an appreciation of these skills, it is next to impossible to ever hope to build any kind of worthwhile relationship with colleagues or customers.

Many people have tried to analyse this complex area of human relations but none has met with more success than the psychologist Abraham Maslow. Basically he discovered that:

- we all have many needs;
- these needs vary in importance;
- we seek to satisfy the most important need first;
- when we have satisfied an important need it ceases to be a motivator;
- we then turn our attention to the next important need.

This is an area so often taken for granted, yet the salesperson who practises the skills of human relations will single himself out from the rest. This chapter should not be interpreted as a comprehensive lesson in these skills, but is merely an introduction.

Common faults in greeting people

- Weak handshakes and bone-crushers.

- Making smart remarks.
- Not looking into people's eyes.
- Making no effort to keep the conversation going.
- Not using the person's name in conversation.
- Talking too softly, too loudly or too much.
- Mumbling.
- Not giving the other person your full attention.
- Ignoring the other person.
- Looking the other person up and down.

The skills of human relations

Admit your mistakes

It is not an expression that we hear too often. Taking responsibility is a very important selling skill. Passing the bucks or cries of 'it's not my fault' are common in our profession. Having the humility to say to a customer 'I'm sorry, I was wrong' or 'It was entirely my fault' is a sign of strength, not weakness, and an admirable quality in a businessperson. Always remember, mistakes are acceptable – excuses never are. Never miss an opportunity to accept responsibility for your own actions.

> **The ability to admit to having made a mistake is the sign of a *good* salesperson.**

Show genuine appreciation

There is not a person in this world who does not want a kind word of appreciation or a sincere compliment. Telling a customer that you have heard great things about him or his company will work wonders for the selling atmosphere, *provided*, of course, that it is true. Showing sincere appreciation to a secretary for typing an urgent report after hours is sometimes more important than extra money in her paypacket.

The power of encouragement

Recognition serves as the greatest means of encouragement. There are few people, if any, who have ever achieved anything worthwhile without the understanding and kindness of someone who believed in them. We would never have heard of the 'Great Caruso' but for his mother, who comforted him when his music teacher told him his voice sounded like 'the wind in the shutters'. We would never have heard of Charles Dickens but for the encouraging words of his first publishers. Another famous author was on the verge of suicide when his teacher told him he had a talent for writing: his name – H.G. Wells.

Consider the power of these statements:

'You really did a great job.'
'You have a very special talent for this kind of work.'
'I like the way you dress; you are always so neat and tidy.'
'I am delighted we are working together on this.'
'I appreciate all your efforts.'
'It's great to have you on the team.'

Seek the opinions of others

Most people like to give an opinion on how certain things can be improved. Asking a customer for his opinion on a new product coming out on the market is sure to get him talking. By seeking the opinions of others we make them feel important and eliminate social and status barriers.

Be cheerful and friendly

Be a comfortable person to be with. Cultivate the quality of being stimulating and interesting so that people will enjoy being in your company. Make a genuine effort to be interested in the pursuits of others and make a definite point of seeing the positive side of their nature.

Give a little extra

Giving customers a little more than they paid for can very often lead to repeat orders. A garage increased its turnover considerably by washing the car and writing on the service docket 'With Compliments'. An estate agent claims that he works entirely off referrals given to him by happy customers. On their first evening in their new home his clients receive flowers, a bottle of wine, a specially prepared meal, the evening papers, local services directory and the temporary use of a portable TV. He maintains that his small investment costs a fraction of what it would cost in advertising and is many times more effective. What opportunities have you got to give that little extra?

Show a little humility

Abraham Lincoln had one quality which separated him from the rest of the statesmen of his time. He was respected by friend and foe alike because of his humility.

In his book *How to Talk Your Way to Success in Selling* Phillip Koerper gives his own definition of the man who has humility:

He has respect for the opinions of others.
He has confidence, but is not overly aggressive.

He is conscious of his own shortcomings.
He is a good listener.
He does not brag or boast.

The value of a smile

Have you ever noticed how hard it is to smile and be angry at the same time? In selling a smile is a very important part of a salesperson's tool kit. It was Confucius who said 'Man without smiling face should not open sweet shop' and a salesperson unable to smile should not be in selling. Considering we use more muscles when we frown than when we smile, it makes us wonder why we do not smile more often.

Be positive and enthusiastic

The sales profession by its very nature will bring you into contact with all types of people. In general they will all have one thing in common – problems. Unknown to ourselves, we can actually depress the customer with remarks like 'Isn't it a lousy day?' or 'I heard that factory up the road is closing down'. While it may be a great way to get the customer talking, it is hardly likely to do anything for his morale. Customers will only buy when they are motivated to do so – not when they are in the depths of depression. It is our role to find solutions to their problems and only an enthusiastic and positive approach will achieve this.

Be courteous

Courtesy is a combination of tolerance, patience, understanding and consideration. It is contagious and is a powerful sales tool. However, too often there is a distinct lack of this important quality. Empty promises such as 'I'll phone you back in 10 minutes' are infuriating, particularly when you are the victim.

Most companies will spend a considerable amount of money advertising their products or service. Yet when the customer rings up or calls in, the salesperson sometimes fails to extend the courtesy and professionalism the customer has been led to expect.

Selling is a highly skilled profession with great emphasis placed on techniques. It is so important however not to lose sight of the fact that this profession is customer-oriented. Basically, we are in the business to solve our customers' problems.

Proof that these skills work

Many people, having attended seminars and sales courses, will write to me and relate some significant event arising out of the use of ideas and skills discussed during the course. Maybe it is only coincidence, but it is significant that most of the letters referred to the successful use of the skills of human relations.

On a personal level, I believe the salesperson who can project humility, warmth and a genuine interest in others will succeed where many will fail. It is for this reason that everybody whose role is to persuade others should try to master the skills. Here are a few examples of how others have used them to their benefit.

Attention to detail can make or break a sale.

- Gerry is a sales executive with a plant machinery company and during his course we discussed the importance of getting people's names right. A few days after the course, he called on a customer, made his presentation and was asked for a quotation in writing. This customer was a Gaelic-speaker and introduced himself by his Gaelic name. Before Gerry submitted the proposal, he made a point of researching the Gaelic spelling of the customer's name. He got the order, which was worth £50,000, and the most significant detail was what the customer said: 'There was little to choose between all three proposals, but I must admit that you were the only one who got my name right!' Moral: If the person has an unusual name, make sure you get it right: you may be the only one who bothered. On the other hand, if your rival gets the name right and you get it wrong, it might cost you the order.

- Here is how the proper use of the skills worked for a college graduate who had attended a sales seminar:

'I arrived at my local squash club to be informed by a stern-looking lady that my membership had expired and I couldn't use the centre until I had paid the £200 annual fee. Not having the money on me I resigned myself to waiting for my friends who had gone to get changed. Without thinking I found myself in conversation with the receptionist and I mentioned that I was thinking of buying a new squash racquet and which type would she advise me to buy. She produced from below the counter her own racquet and gave me a complete rundown on the benefits of this particular type. I must have impressed her with my interest because she suggested that I should try it and I said I would, just as soon as I paid my fee. She insisted that I should forget about the fee for that night. I had an entertaining evening free of charge. When I thought about it afterwards, I was convinced that her change of attitude was a direct result of asking her advice.

The sequel to this story is that since then she has become my lawyer, my doctor, my career guidance teacher, my priest and a host of other people and I never miss an opportunity to ask her advice or opinion on anything. I have been playing there for six months and I still haven't paid my fee!'

- Martin was another person who wrote to me. He had been thinking of buying a camera, so he had approached a photographer friend and asked for his advice on making a purchase. The photographer produced a camera and gave him full details on why this was the right one. He spent one hour explaining how it worked and then to Martin's astonishment he was handed the camera and told to keep it as a present. He estimated that the camera was worth about £300. Was Martin one of the few people who had made the photographer feel important by asking for his advice?

- Susan, a former delegate on a training course, walked into a department store looking for a job as a senior salesperson. This store was notorious for giving all job-seekers the standard response 'Send in a copy of your CV'. Susan decided to take it a stage further and spoke to the personnel manager by phone from the floor of the department store, saying 'I would really appreciate about two minutes of your time, I need to get your opinion on something.' She was ushered up to his office and greeted him with: 'Thank you for seeing me, Mr Bushe. You are an expert in how people should put their curriculum vitae together: I would appreciate your advice on how mine could be improved.' She got the job!

There is obviously something in our nature that makes us feel good when others come to us for help. Asking others for opinions and advice has worked wonders for many people, and I could relate many more stories of the effect of exercising good human relations. Another story I must relate is one that I would consider a classic:

- A former trainee who had set up his own sandwich express got an idea that what he required to improve delivery of his service was an electric van of the sort commonly used for bread and milk

Dial-A-Sandwich
Any Street
Anytown

Mr Peter Wayne
Managing Director
Superslices Ltd
Anytown

Dear Mr Wayne,

I am a new user of your products, which are an essential element in my business, which is delivering meals, mainly at lunchtime. I started by calling to your bakery at 6.30 a.m. daily, but now your van calls to my door and I am enjoying weekly credit facilities at wholesale rates. I am deeply grateful for this support, but must further acknowledge that some of the praise for my product is rightly due to the fresh consistency of the bread and rolls you deliver to me.

I have now launched my own business and can state with certainty that there is a strong demand for the service. Already I have three people working for me plus one part-timer on the phone. I can identify significant potential in this market and feel that my management problem is to expand in an orderly way. Presently, I am resisting the temptation to expand too quickly because I want to give a consistently good service and maintain the quality of the product.

Transport and delivery are crucial factors for orderly growth and this is an area where I make bold to suggest that the great and established Superslices could co-operate with the newly born Dial-A-Sandwich in the cause of mutual profitability. Under some form of lenient franchise or rental system could Dial-A-Sandwich use one of your battery-operated vans for the distribution of my product, which is also yours? Would you have an old vehicle in need of refurbishment which could be sold to me on easy terms – very easy terms? Would it be possible to meet you, Sir, to discuss this matter?

On Saturday night the Prime Minister appealed for innovation in job creation. I am giving Dial-A-Sandwich my best shot and with some help it can blossom into a thriving cashflow business.

What can I do for Superslices? We have little labels which we stick onto each item. In time we could have printed onto them this legend: 'We only use the best – Superslices'. If the van were made available under responsible terms and conditions, the sides of the vehicle could blazon forth the same message. Our leaflets could also conform to the same marketing concept.

My sincere thanks for your help and co-operation so far. I hope we have a great future together! I enclose a copy of the leaflets which we distribute presently and my CV, just for the record.

Yours sincerely,

Jonathan Jones
Dial-A-Sandwich

PS: Thanks to your staff for the courtesy with which they have treated me.

deliveries. Not having much capital, he hoped that he might be able to persuade his local bread supplier to part with one that needed repair for a small investment. He wrote a letter (see p. 54) which I reprint with his kind permission. (The names and locations have been changed to avoid embarrassment.)

One week after sending the letter, Jonathan received a phone call inviting him in. Peter Wayne greeted him warmly and thanked him for his letter. He brought him over to the window, pointed to a van parked in the yard and asked him whether that one would do. Jonathan agreed with sheer delight. He was handed the keys and a release order for a battery. When he asked what terms he was getting it under, he was told 'It's yours, and best of luck to you in your new business.' Jonathan subsequently informed me that the approximate value of the van and the battery was £3,000.

It goes without saying that Jonathan was fortunate, but the story makes the point: if you ask in the proper manner, anything is possible!

Techniques for improving your memory

One point that comes up constantly on training courses, from people in all sectors of industry, is the inability to remember people's names. While there are many ways to improve memory, unless you can convince people that they don't have a bad memory in the first place, it is unlikely they will believe any technique will work.

Good memory is a skill which can be learned.

There is no such thing as a bad memory, just an untrained one. According to memory experts, if at the age of 21 you were to write down everything you could possibly remember about your past experience it would take you approximately 2,500 years. Not bad for an average memory.

It would not be possible to go into all the techniques of memory improvement in this chapter, and many books on the subject are available. One that comes to mind is *Memory Magic* by Harry Lorrayne.

The use of mnemonics
A mnemonic is an aid to memory. If you wanted to know how many days there are in April you would probably recite 'Thirty days hath September, April, June and November ...'. That is what is known as a mnemonic. If you were asked to name the five great lakes, the word 'Homes' will give great assistance: H – Huron; O – Ontario; M – Michigan; E – Erie; S – Superior. People use mnemonics to assist in

public speaking and they are particularly helpful to anybody trying to remember vital information. For salespeople AIDA has always stood for Attention, Interest, Desire and Action – the steps involved in negotiating a sale. On training programmes the use of mnemonics is encouraged because it not only aids learning but also reinforces the message. In many cases these mnemonics are never forgotten.

The calendar system

Let us start by improving your ability to remember dates. By learning twelve digits in sequence you have a mental calendar for the year. Let us take 1989 as an example. Study these numbers and learn them in the proper sequence. The best way to do it is to learn three first, then six, nine and finally twelve.

2	6	6
3	1	5
3	7	4
2	6	4

Once these numbers are indelibly implanted in your brain, you have a calendar for 1989. Each of these 12 numbers represents the first Monday of a month of 1989: 2, 6, 6 represent January, February and March: 3, 1, 5 represent April, May and June; and so on. Suppose you were seeking to establish what day 8th March was, for example: you know that the first Monday is the 6th, so the 8th must be a Wednesday. It should take no more than ten minutes to learn the system completely. You can have great fun at parties demonstrating your incredible feats of memory. Use the same system for other years: the sequence of numbers will change from year to year, but will repeat itself in year eight.

As a memory test, try to remember the following list of 14 words:

Open-mindedness	Common Sense	Manners
Names	Illustration	Courtesy
Simplicity	Understanding	Observation
Memory	Tolerance	Integrity
Naturalness	Attitude	

Without reading any further, how many can you remember? Was it difficult to remember 4, 10 or the entire 14? Now, without looking back at the list, write down the word 'communications' and use each letter as an aid to remembering the 14 words. There should be a marked improvement. If I am giving a talk on communications, all I need is that mnemonic and I have all the material I require for that session.

The 'link' system of memory

Have a look at the following list of objects and then close the book and see how many you can remember in their proper sequence.

orange
lighthouse
ballroom
deckchairs
camera
table lamp
balloon
washing machine
ladder
soap powder

In order for memory skills to work everything must be exaggerated out of all proportion. The bigger, more colourful and more amusing the idea, the more chance you have of remembering it. Try to remember these objects by using the 'link' method.

First of all, visualise an *orange*, the biggest that you have ever seen, give it as much detail as you possibly can and have it standing on the floor in front of you, pushing up against the ceiling. Next imagine cutting into the orange and finding inside it a *lighthouse* with lights flashing and the waves crashing into the surrounding rocks. Make the picture as vivid as possible. See yourself walking inside the lighthouse and you see the biggest *ballroom* that you've ever seen; hear the music, see the people. As you look around you begin to notice two *deckchairs*, the biggest you have ever seen, dancing with one another and people are standing around applauding them and taking photographs with *cameras*. Look at these amazing cameras flashing, thousands of them. But then you notice that the flashes on the cameras are unusual: they are all *table lamps*, switching on and off each time they take a picture. Suddenly all the cameras and the table lamps explode and everything mushrooms into a massive *balloon* with all its colours. When the balloon hits the ceiling it bursts in a loud bang and out of it come thousands of *washing machines*, floating slowly towards the ground. You walk up to the washing machines, which are twice your size, and climb on a *ladder* to look inside. Your feet keep slipping off the ladder as you try to look into the washing machine and you end up in a sea of *soap powder*.

Now write all the words down in their proper sequence without reading back.

Most people find that they can remember every one of them with little difficulty. You may never need to use this system but practising it helps your confidence in memory retention and that is one of the more important aspects of developing a powerful memory.

Hints on remembering people's names

The ability to remember people's names and to use them is an important skill, not only in human relations but also in selling. Consider the following statement: 'I understand why you might say that, Peter – however ...'. If you read that aloud and repeat it without using the name, the effect will not be the same.

The importance of using people's proper names in conversation can never be underestimated. One American newspaper considers it so important to get the person's name right that the journalists lose a day's pay for spelling the name wrong.

The following are eight helpful hints on remembering people's names:

1. Be totally conscious of the importance of remembering names.
2. When introduced to someone, make sure that you hear the name properly.
3. Don't be embarrassed about asking people to repeat or spell their names. Most people will be pleased that you were interested enough to ask.
4. Use the person's name as often as is appropriate during discussion.
5. Repeat the name to yourself during the conversation.
6. On parting, use the name again.
7. Most important of all, having met new acquaintances, mentally review their names when you get a quiet moment.
8. Practise remembering the names of people who work with your customer, such as receptionists and secretaries.

15 ways to get along with others

(These are equally relevant to your relations with family, friends, acquaintances, colleagues and customers.)

1. Make a conscious decision to start liking people. Look for their more positive points. People's better traits are like the 'iceberg principle', hidden beneath the surface.

2. Separate people's irritating behaviour from their personality. Recognise that it is their behaviour that you find irritating – not them.

3. Be conscious of the difference between a punishment and a correction. A punishment is given in public with the intention of humiliating. A correction is given in private with calmness and sincerity and with the intention of helping the offender.

4. If you must knock somebody else's idea, do it gently, never maliciously and then only when you can come up with a better one yourself.

5. Never make cheap remarks about people less fortunate than yourself. Avoid gossip and back-stabbing. Try to create an atmosphere in which others never feel threatened or manipulated.

6. Never miss an opportunity to say something positive to others on their achievement, no matter how small or insignificant it may appear. Avoid being a John Blunt, the painter of the worst picture.

7. Never back down from a commitment. Promises made should be kept, regardless of cost or personal embarrassment.

8. Develop a genuine interest in the pursuits and difficulties of others. Work hard at eliminating social and status barriers and avoid bragging about your own personal achievements.

9. Make a point of being tolerant. It's nice to be important but more important to be nice. Bring others into the 'team' by asking their advice and opinions.

10. Be upright and honest in your dealings. Let others know that they are dealing with someone they can trust. Develop a reputation for being fair and just in your appraisal of others.

11. Show by example and never expect others to do what you wouldn't do yourself. Avoid comparing one with another and don't expect anybody to imitate the ideals of another.

12. Never condemn, criticise or complain to anybody for making a mistake. Demonstrate the education to be derived from having blundered.

13. Be a comfortable person to be with. Cultivate the quality of being stimulated and interesting and remember that a smile is the shortest distance between two people.

14. Learn and use the names of supposedly unimportant people. Try to 'catch them doing something right'. Compliment and encourage often but avoid flattery at all costs.

15. Make a definite decision to start improving your social skills and complete the following exercise.

HUMAN RELATIONS – PERSONAL APPRAISAL

In completing this exercise, write down in the area provided all the skills, talents and personal qualities you like and dislike in other people. Work on the basis that, if others have traits that get your back up and you have the same traits, it would be wise to eliminate them. On the other hand, if others have qualities that you admire or respect, identify and start trying to develop them.

Motivating qualities	Demotivating qualities

1. Put a tick against each quality that you consider you possess.
2. Highlight the areas you would like to develop or accentuate.
3. Highlight the negative qualities you wish to eliminate.
4. Transfer these qualities to your Personal Development Plan.

PERSONAL DEVELOPMENT

Positives to develop	Negatives to eliminate
1.	1.
2.	2.
3.	3.
4.	4.
5.	5.
6.	6.
7.	7.
8.	8.
9.	9.
10.	10.
11.	11.
12.	12.
13.	13.
14.	14.
15.	15.
16.	16.
17.	17.
18.	18.
19.	19.
20.	20.

◀ CHAPTER 4 ▶

CUSTOMER CARE

Maintaining sales through better customer service

In the selling world, the customer appears twice: as a consumer in the market and as part of the after-sales service system. It is on the harmony between these two aspects of the relationship that the customer will evaluate your company.

The customer will assess your company on its liaison between these two aspects of the relationship.

When I talk to salespeople about after-sales service, they say, 'If those people back in head office only realised how difficult it is to get the order in the first place, they might be a little more supportive.' When I talk to the service department they respond with, 'It's OK for him to talk about support. If he quoted realistic delivery dates we wouldn't be under so much pressure.' This kind of interminable bickering results in customer irritation and an eventual loss of business.

To be successful in the marketplace it is important to be 'positively different'. According to the experts, and by that I mean the buyers, if a company demonstrates it can provide top-quality service consistently it will be successful in any market conditions.

It is not acceptable for any company to be selective in the manner in which it greets callers to its offices. We have all had the experience of being treated with something less than courtesy during a sales approach to a company. Do these people not realise that the person who is trying to sell to them today may be a prospective customer tomorrow? How many suppliers have been left resentful after continual hassles trying to get payment for a long-outstanding invoice? The plus factor about customer service is that courtesy to *everybody* establishes a style of company behaviour which enhances the company's image. Courtesy attracts repeat business while bad manners repel. It is as simple as this: *everybody* in your company sells! The managing director who does not take calls from the troubled customer and delegates all matters to junior management will damage the image of the company. The superior-sounding secretary who demands, 'What's it in connection with?' will do little to develop harmonious relationships. The insensitive accounts clerk who writes threatening letters and uses the old cliché 'We are not a bank' will not be forgotten. The uncaring sales clerk who promises everything and delivers nothing will do untold damage and so will the delivery crew if they drive over the customer's best roses.

Most companies invest heavily in sales teams to win business but inefficient back-up and insensitive attitudes to marketing will squander these gains. The ironic factor is that the employees involved are paid good money while losing business. This is a vital area for management, which must ensure that nobody operates outside the parameters of selling.

Business is lost not only between nine and five. It can be lost in the evenings or at the weekends. A customer told me that he had decided to put in some aluminium windows for his house and he had decided on one particular company. Late one Saturday evening he was driving carefully out of the city when an inconsiderate van-driver flashed his lights, blew his horn and made aggressive gestures. Blinded by the headlights, my customer pulled over to let the van pass. As he did so the other driver gave him a two-finger greeting. However, the car owner noticed the name on the van. It was the window company with which he had been doing business. In spite of all the gracious apologies offered by the salesperson, his company did not get the business.

Bad news travels fast and the business world is not a metropolis where nobody knows anybody: it's a village – a village run by people who talk to other people. There is a 'bad news circle' of about 200 people that may eventually hear of *one* bad experience that you have had. Everyone will have indirect communication with those 200 people and if the news is bad enough all 200 will hear it! Someone put it in a nutshell when he said, 'When I do something wrong, everybody knows about it; when I do something right, nobody is around to see me doing it.'

Everybody who contacts your company should be treated with warmth, kindness and consideration because it may pay big dividends. Is your company run by people who leave customers standing around or holding on at the other end of a telephone? What are the implications of doing so? If a taxi-driver and a salesperson arrive at reception who will wait the longer, and why?

A few years ago, not long after I had started in the training business, I was doing some canvassing on a miserably wet day. It was the kind of weather in which people don't even put milk bottles out. I called on a business equipment company whose warmth and hospitality were much appreciated, even though they were not in the market for my services at that time. Twelve months later, my business had expanded to the extent that I required a word processor and a copier. I attended a business equipment exhibition, toured the stands and found it difficult to separate one company's products from another until a familiar figure came over to greet me. He was the person who had rescued me from my travelling blues on a miserable day 12 months previously. I had no further difficulty in deciding to whom the £6,000 order was going. I made a point of telling them that their friendly treatment was ultimately responsible for placing the order.

Look after your customers and they will look after you.

Staff attitudes to customers play a big part in the continuing business relationship: it is critical that everybody in the organisation is constantly vigilant in the matter of public relations.

Recently, on a trip to the US, I stayed in a number of places where I found hotels had incentive schemes to encourage patrons to use the accommodation facilities of the entire chain of hotels. One such group is the Radisson. As I entered the hotel I noticed that all the staff (including the manager) were wearing badges with 'Yes, I can' written on them. I discovered also that all communications with patrons started with 'Yes, I can' or 'How can I help you?' Some people may characterise this as typically American gimmickry but being on the receiving end of the benefits of efficient and bubbly service, I was impressed by the performance. It may have been some kind of 'psychological motivator' but it worked, and it's the end product that counts. It would be difficult for staff members to start a conversation with 'Yes, I can' and then make liars out of themselves by saying 'I am sorry, that is not possible'. If we could all greet customers with such positive mental attitudes (not necessarily verbalised) the impact on the growth of the business would be dynamic.

Taking all these points into consideration, let us examine some of the many reasons why business is lost *after* the prospective buyer has been converted into a customer.

Why customers stop buying

Dun & Bradstreet carried out the following survey, which revealed some interesting information. It showed that 16% of buyers will stop buying every year for the following reasons:

1% die
3% change jobs or move away
5% favour friends
9% change for better prices
82% are unhappy with suppliers

There may be little we can do to save the first 18% but the other 82% is well within the capability of most organisations. By retrieving them you not only help to swell company profits but you are also securing your own job.

Why customers are unhappy with their suppliers

In competitive markets customers have a choice. If we cannot give them what they are looking for, they can always get it somewhere else. These are some of the factors that customers find irritating when making contact for service:

Product
- products not delivered when agreed
- parts missing when delivered
- parts not in stock
- too long to get service or parts
- product inadequate for intended use
- referred back to manufacturer when something goes wrong

Service
- response time too slow
- service not given when promised
- lack of urgency or understanding by service department
- no follow-up by salespeople or company

Faults when phoning the supplier

- phone not answered promptly

- company not properly identified
- the standard 'Who's calling?'
- uninterested, bored or impatient voice
- a 'little girl' voice
- every question responded to with 'Just a moment, please'
- unexplained interruptions
- long periods of silence
- abrupt or aimless transfers
- requests for message to be repeated
- ignorance of whereabouts of company personnel and their movements
- the 'He's in a meeting at the moment' lie
- The 'He will phone you back in five minutes' lie
- hanging up before the customer does
- carrying on two conversations at the same time.

Your company's reputation is in the hands of the first person to pick up the telephone. Countless business opportunities are lost by not picking up messages, queries or sales leads. If this type of problem exists in your company, bring it to the attention of somebody who will listen. Sometimes it's an idea to phone your own company to find out how difficult it is for others to make contact and what information is forthcoming.

Attitude projected by supplier's staff

When visiting or phoning internal staff:

- don't seem to care, 'I only work here' attitude
- cold, unfriendly manner
- person in authority not available
- false promises or lack of real interest
- not listening properly
- buck-passing, 'I'll pass on the message'
- defensive attitude, 'It's not my fault'
- not coming back when promised
- rudeness, arguing or insinuating that the customer is wrong
- insufficient knowledge to assist the customer
- indecisive: 'I'll try', 'I think' or 'Maybe'
- interrupting the customer

- lack of courtesy
- getting too technical
- no action taken
- senior management making themselves unavailable

When internal staff are challenged on their attitude towards customers they invariably become defensive. Many say 'I wasn't rude', 'I was not unhelpful' and so on. Even though this may be true *it is the customer's perception that matters.* The customers may be wrong every time, but we cannot let them think that. Remember, it is the customer who ultimately pays your salary.

Welcoming people into your company

1. Look the person in the eye.

2. Smile warmly.

3. Greet him with a friendly 'Good morning/afternoon. Welcome.'

4. Say 'How can I help you?' Avoid 'Can I help you?' – it's boring and monotonous and sometimes conveys 'What the hell are you doing here?'

5. Question skilfully and wait until the person explains the purpose of the call. Not everybody is capable of explaining precisely what he is looking for and he may need help.

6. Briefly summarise the visitor's request to ensure that you have got the message correctly. Get the caller's name and use it.

7. Avoid saying 'We haven't got one in stock', 'He is not available', 'We don't sell them any more' without offering a realistic alternative.

8. Explain what you are going to do and how long it will take, if appropriate.

9. If possible, offer the visitor coffee or a newspaper. This keeps him

away from the counter or reception area and allows others to get on with their work.

10. Don't leave visitors in the dark. If the request is taking longer than anticipated, tell them and keep them informed of progress.

11. When your business is completed, give them your name so that they can get back to a person not a department, if they have any further queries.

12. Few people do it but it makes such a difference to say: 'Thank you for the business, Mr/Mrs ... Please come back and see us again.' It does wonders for the parting impression.

Handling complaints and arguments

Everybody knows that you cannot *win* an argument, yet so many people try. Salespeople come into contact with many different people every day. Those people will have their day brightened or darkened by the manner, attitude and tone of the salesperson's greeting or communication skills. It is unwise to be drawn into verbal conflict for the following reasons:

- Arguments leave both parties beaten and drained and the subsequent atmosphere is rarely conducive to selling or good communications.
- Even if you win, you lose – if not the motivation, respect and support of colleagues and friends, quite likely the sale and possibly one of your best customers.
- An argument is a challenge to another person's 'emotional judgement' and you will never change somebody's opinion once you have challenged that judgement.

Five attitudes to the customer's complaint
1. Don't expect the customer to be in a rational frame of mind. Complaints provoke emotion.

2. Maintain a professional approach. The customer is likely to be oversensitive to a casual or uncaring attitude.

3. Complaints are an opportunity to demonstrate the high standards of professionalism of your company.

4. Don't pass the buck. Take personal responsibility to ensure that the complaint or query is met to the customer's satisfaction.

5. Show that you really do care.

The ability to communicate another point of view to a person who is highly emotional is a very important skill. It can be acquired and here is one way of doing it that works. Regardless of how emotional – or placid – the other person may be, the same rules apply.

1. *Listen, listen, listen*
   A most important skill in handling conflict is the ability to listen with all your senses. Avoid trying to calm the other person down, this will only make the situation worse.

2. *Remain calm*
   Try to maintain your cool. Ensure that your body language or telephone reaction is not conveying anger or shock. This will encourage the other person to get it all 'off his chest'. Don't allow yourself to be drawn into an argument.

3. *Never interrupt*
   Apart from being the height of bad manners, it will only add to the other person's annoyance.

4. *Respond when appropriate*
   Use expressions like 'I see', 'I understand', or 'I agree'.

5. *Ask appropriate questions*
   The only way you can demonstrate your 'real interest' in another's point of view is to ask questions. Take notes as you go along for the purpose of summarising when appropriate. Ask open-ended questions such as 'why?', 'what?', 'when?' etc.

6. *Ignore insults*
   When people are angry they occasionally say things that they really don't mean. Customers may say something like 'I've already told

you that, are you deaf?' or 'How stupid you people are!' It is very easy to take these comments personally, but nothing is to be gained from drawing a new issue into the discussion. When the situation is resolved the customer will usually apologise for his remarks. Ignore the insults and ask some appropriate question about the main issue. Developing this skill requires patience and tremendous self-discipline but it's worth it.

7. *Wait for calmness*
Experience indicates that people can't shout at the top of their voices forever – they will eventually calm down. Usually, your courtesy in listening will be reciprocated. If the other person interrupts you, it probably means that you haven't given him enough time to explain himself. In any event try to avoid embarrassing the other person with the age-old 'political' cliché: 'I didn't interrupt you so please don't interrupt me.'

8. *Summarise the points at issue*
Demonstrate your understanding of the issues by summarising with: 'If I understand you correctly this is the situation. . . .' Ensure that the customer agrees with your interpretation.

Empathy is the word for understanding without necessarily agreeing. Bearing in mind that the complaint may be based on a lack of information on the customer's part, telling him he is wrong or that you don't agree is not likely to help an already difficult situation. Empathy is expressed thus:

> 'I can understand how you feel about it, Mr Smith, and if I were in that situation I am sure I would be just as annoyed; however, there is another view that I would ask you to consider. . . .'

There should never be a case where a salesperson should have to use 'I disagree with you' or 'We will have to agree to differ'. By mentioning 'disagreement' you are highlighting the fact that you are in conflict.

9. *Find an area of agreement and state it*
It will be a rare case where a customer will have it so wrong that there will be no areas for agreement. Even conceding a small point may add to a conciliatory atmosphere. Something like: 'Mr Smith,

I agree with you – if we said we would deliver on Tuesday and you didn't receive it until Thursday, that is totally unacceptable and I would be just as angry.' Alternatively, if you or your company are at fault for the entire complaint, apologise, get it out of the way and take the appropriate action. Customers accept and expect things to go wrong now and then: the critical point is how the complaint is handled.

10. *Demonstrate empathy*
Customers don't always expect us to agree with them but what all of them can justifiably expect is that we will do our utmost to understand their point of view.

11. *Agree on action*
Whatever agreement is made between you and the customer should be followed up with all haste. Complaints are an acceptable part of business but how they are handled will dictate your future relationship with the customer.

12. *Thank the customer for the complaint*

Complaints are opportunities or problems depending on how you approach them.

The customer has a choice: to bring the complaint to you or to your competitor. Those that bring their complaints directly to you should be thanked. Sometimes a brief note to the customer thanking him for taking the time to contact you and giving you the opportunity to correct the problem will do a lot for the business relationship. Many people protest by taking their business elsewhere.

Some hints on handling overdue accounts

Every so often salespeople have to collect an overdue account. This is not the most pleasing part of the salesperson's role but one that is best carried out by people who have the company's relationship with the customer in mind.

Debt collection demands very sensitive customer handling.

Overdue accounts are a sensitive area for both the supplier and the customer. The business relationship may be at risk if the approach to collecting the money is not carried out professionally. This vital part of customer communication can be enhanced by observing some important points:

1. *Stress credit policy at the time of the order*
   If salespeople take the time to explain credit policy when taking the order it eliminates a lot of unnecessary dialogue between the two accounts departments. Many salespeople are vague when it comes to payment: they say, 'We will send you an invoice', without following it up with 'Our payment terms are strictly 30 days: is that acceptable to you, Mr Smith?'

   If a commitment is made to the salesperson by the customer, the experience is usually that few problems arise.

2. *How to deal with a customer who constantly ignores credit terms*
   When a salesperson is trying to collect money from a customer, that is not the time to give him a lecture over his abuse of the credit system.

   There are two issues to be considered: one is collecting the money and the other is educating the customer regarding future payments. Each of these issues should be addressed in isolation. Collect the money when you can and in whatever diplomatic way you see fit. When it comes to asking the customer to pay within the credit terms, do it when the money is *not* due and you may get a more sympathetic hearing.

3. *Be in touch with all the facts*
   Some customers are notorious for querying invoices. Ensure that all queries have been addressed prior to your telephone call or visit.

4. *Analyse possible reasons for non-payment*
   Oversight? Notoriously slow? Outstanding query? Change of address?

5. *Discuss with person in authority*
   Get the name and title of the people who sign the cheques and try to talk to them. Discussion of your business with junior staff members is likely to lead to frustration. If you have no success with them try enlisting the help of the person who gave you the order. In many cases he is unaware of your difficulty and can be most helpful, particularly if you have been a good supplier.

6. *How to talk to a person in authority*
   If the customer is in breach of his commitment to pay within the credit terms, you have every right to enquire as to the reasons for

73

non-payment. It is important to be polite and friendly, while at the same time asserting your commitment to gaining payment.

When speaking to the contact, one of these reasons will usually be given:

- 'The cheque is in the post.' Ask when the cheque can be expected and thank the customer.
- 'The cheque is waiting for a second signature.' Impress on the customer the importance of getting in the cheque. Ask when the other signatory will be available and arrange to call to collect it.
- 'There is a query on this invoice.' If you have done your homework properly, this should not prove to be an insurmountable obstacle. If it is a delaying tactic, ask the customer to pay the amount that is not in dispute. If a mistake is confirmed immediately, say: 'If I get a credit note to you today, may I arrange for somebody to collect a cheque tomorrow afternoon?'
- 'No money is available at the moment.' Use empathetic expressions like: 'We well understand the problem you face in getting the money in these days – we have the same problem ourselves'; 'You are normally so prompt with your payment'; or 'We greatly appreciate the business you place with us.' Regardless of the reasons never let a customer away without a firm commitment to pay.
- 'I'll check it out and phone you back in five minutes.' The customer is in the driving seat if he takes the initiative in making the vital call. Tell him there is a lot of pressure on your telephone line and he may not get through. Suggest that you will phone him instead.

7. *Getting the 'runaround'*
   If a customer owes money you have every right to exert whatever diplomatic pressure is necessary. Some people are past masters at making themselves 'unavailable' and they require a more aggressively imaginative approach. Some of the following suggestions may be required only in very severe circumstances. Remember, if you can't make contact with the signatory who is making it difficult for you, you can't get your money. In these circumstances you may consider any of the following ideas, which have achieved success for others.

- Send the customer a telex or fax, stressing how difficult it has been to contact him.
- Phone the customer at home. (Many credit card companies are doing this.)
- Call at his home.
- Write to him at home.
- Arrange to bump into him 'by chance' first thing in the morning as he comes into his office.
- Phone his secretary and leave a message for him to contact you. The only details you give are your first name and an unlisted phone number, stressing that it is 'very urgent'.

In using any of these techniques, be prepared for an aggressive response from the customers, although sometimes he or she can become polite when embarrassed. It is recommended that these actions should be used only when all else has failed.

8. *Cheque not received when promised*
   Phone the customer to politely express surprise that payment still has not been received. Apply a little extra pressure. Say something like 'While I'm on, Mr Smith, would you mind checking when that payment went out?'

9. *Always thank the customer*
   Regardless of the outcome of your discussions, always thank the customer for his time. Courtesy costs nothing, yet achieves so much.

Responding to punctual payment
Companies will spend a fortune reminding customers they have not paid their bills. Yet few, if any, invest the cost of a telephone call to thank a customer for prompt payment. One can only guess the extent of the good will gained by such an inexpensive exercise.

What is a customer?

- A customer is the most important person ever to contact us – in person, by mail or by telephone.
- A customer is not dependent on us – we are dependent on him.
- A customer is not an interruption of our work – he is the purpose of it.

- We are not doing the customer a favour by serving him – he is doing us a favour by allowing us to fulfil that function.
- Customers are not cold statistics, they are human beings with feelings and emotions like our own.
- A customer is not someone with whom to match wits. Nobody ever won an argument with a customer.
- Customers are people who bring their wants and needs. It is our job to cater for them, thereby profiting the customer and our company.

Customer service PRACTICE

Good customer service is summed up in the word PRACTICE:

Promptness	Prepared and willing to be of service.
Reliability	Trustworthy, deserving of complete confidence.
Accuracy	The ability to observe and act with precision.
Courtesy	The ability to be gracious, obliging and polite.
Tactfulness	The ability to say the right thing without offence.
Information	The communication of knowledge or education.
Competence	The ability and capacity to carry out a task.
Empathy	Emotional or intellectual identification with another.

Promptness
Respond to phone, mail and personal visits with minimum delay. Goods or services promised should be despatched with all haste. Be quick to do whatever is necessary to inspire confidence. The company's image is reflected by the manner in which you conduct yourself.

Reliability
Promises made must be kept, regardless of cost or inconvenience. Reliability is conveyed through action, not by promises. Reliable service reflects professionalism, sincerity and efficiency. If you are unable to assist, try to find an acceptable alternative. We rarely get a second chance to demonstrate our reliability.

Accuracy
Ensure that all information is accurate, complete and up to date. Note all the relevant facts of a customer's query, particularly names. If a

mistake has been made, accept responsibility and solve the problem. Read back the customer's query to demonstrate your understanding. Avoid slang or technical jargon. Communicate on the customer's wavelength.

Courtesy

Identify yourself, be polite, respond when appropriate and listen. Give the customer your undivided attention and use his name often. Be yourself. Falseness breeds mistrust and insincerity. Courtesy is contagious. So are aggression and bad manners. Your tone, manner and speech convey your personality. Be enthusiastic.

Tactfulness

If a request cannot be granted, explain why and do not make excuses. Disregard insults. Do not get personally involved. Maintain voice control. Speak with conviction and sincerity – this will help to assure the customer. Be as helpful, friendly and good-humoured as the situation allows.

Information

Customers expect you to have detailed knowledge of your company. Keep the customer informed of your progress. Do not keep him in the dark. Keep the customer informed of any new circumstances that affect him. Check all customer queries on the spot and respond accordingly. Do not pass on hearsay; ensure that all information is accurate and complete.

Competence

Convince the customer that he is dealing with someone who *can* solve his problem. Avoid such phrases as 'I will try', 'I think', 'maybe' or 'it should be'. Do not pass the blame on to someone else: this angers the customer. Speak in a manner that suggests maturity, knowledge and action. If you have a solution, explain what you *will* do and do it.

Empathy

Listen carefully to the customer's story and never interrupt. Put yourself in the customer's place. Do you *really* understand? Encourage customers to bring complaints to you, not to your competitor. Do not expect the customer to be reasonable: complaints provoke emotion. Express regret for the problem, be sympathetic and take *immediate* action.

The following is a list of questions that should indicate your personal level of 'customer care':

1. If you got a sales lead and a customer complaint simultaneously, which one would you handle first?

2. If you promised a customer delivery on Friday and you subsequently discovered that his order would not be delivered until the following Tuesday, would you phone him before Friday to tell him or would you wait until he complained?

3. Do you write to customers after a visit only to thank them for business they have given you?

4. Do you communicate to the customer who complains that you really do care?

5. When you promise 'outstanding service' are you speaking on (a) your own behalf, (b) your company's behalf or (c) both? If (b) or (c), do you do all you can to ensure that the customer's perception of 'service' is upheld?

Phrases to avoid

We will all agree that the selling atmosphere between ourselves and the customer is of tremendous importance. Anything that adds to or takes away from that atmosphere must be considered. When dealing at customer service level the last thing we want to do is get the customer more annoyed than he or she already is. A minor query can turn into a serious complaint if any of the company's staff members say the wrong thing at the wrong time.

Over the past few years I have collected a number of offending phrases common to businesses involved in selling goods and services.

● *Can I help you?*
The most predictable of all greetings and used by practically everybody involved in customer contact. This statement puts pressure on prospective buyers to make a decision the moment they walk in the door. The usual response is: 'No thank you, I am just looking around.' Any further pressure by the salesperson, in their manner or by questioning, will

result in the buyer walking out. 'How can I help you?' takes the pressure off the buyer and will create a better atmosphere. Some stores have become aware of the dangers of the 'Can I help you?' syndrome and have replaced it with:

'Good morning, you are very welcome. May I be of service or do you wish to browse around?'

This gives the prospective buyer a choice and, even though he will most likely take the 'look around' option, he will be more receptive to suggestions from the salesperson subsequently.

- *With all due respect...*

This is normally used in response to some critical remark made by the customer. 'With all due respect' really means 'thinking very little of you, as I do' and is usually associated with some body language that confirms the salesperson's irritation. Next time you hear or use the statement, observe the subsequent remarks and body language of both people and I believe you will see at least 'polite aggression'.

- *I hope this doesn't go over your head...*
- *Without getting too technical...*
- *To put this in simple terms...*

The buyer's interpretation could be: 'As you haven't got the intelligence to understand this, I shall explain it in such a way that even an imbecile like you will find it hard to miss the point.'

Recently, when co-presenting a sales seminar, my colleague started his presentation with: 'To ensure that this doesn't go over your heads....' Later that day (after he had departed) a number of people told me how offended they were by his statement. They did not tell him they were annoyed – they told me.

In the interests of diplomacy it might be a good idea to use such expressions as: 'I hope I can explain myself properly...'

- *I hope I am not boring you.*
- *Without boring you any further...*

If somebody says, 'Don't think of a white horse', what do you think of? A white horse of course. When we say to a customer, 'I hope I'm not boring you', we are suggesting to the customer that he is bored – and if not, he should be.

- *You've got me wrong.*
- *That is not what I said.*
- *You have misinterpreted me.*

It is not a good idea to blame customers for our inability to put ourselves across. It is more diplomatic to accept responsibility for the communication breakdown with: 'I'm sorry, I'm not explaining myself properly.'

- *This is not a cricitism...*
- *Now don't take offence...*
- *I am not knocking them... but ...*
- *I am not complaining but...*
- *I am not interrupting you but...*

Every time somebody says 'this is not a criticism' they proceed to tear the other person to pieces. When we say, 'don't take offence' we proceed to offend. People try to defend these statements by suggesting that criticisms are helpful if they are 'constructive'. I have never known anybody to feel good about criticism and the only person who can decide if it is constructive or not is the receiver.

Some people offer 'help' in the form of a criticism and their 'help' is misinterpreted. I am of the opinion that the word 'criticism' should be totally eliminated from our vocabulary. Replace 'criticism' with 'observation', and you will find more willing listeners because calling something an 'observation' does not imply that the subsequent comments are going to be hurtful.

I have asked hundreds of people which they would prefer, a 'criticism' or an 'observation'. All agreed that using the word 'observation' implied that what was to follow was helpful. By contrast, people saying that they are 'not knocking' or 'not complaining' or 'not interrupting' are about to do just that.

- *You are entitled to your opinion.*
- *I disagree with you.*

Normally said when the salesperson is under pressure from the customer's disagreeable attitude and likely to add further fuel to the fire. By mentioning that we 'disagree' we are highlighting the fact that we are in 'conflict' which is the last thing that we wish to do. There is an old expression that goes as follows: 'You will never change a man's opinion once you have challenged his judgement.' I believe that that is also true in selling.

Buyers like to feel that their point of view is valid, and if credit is given for that view they will be more receptive to an opposite viewpoint. If we are to learn from the experts, we should explain ourselves with something resembling the following:

'That's a very interesting point of view, Mr Smith, and I can understand why you feel that way – in fact, I was talking to a customer the other day and he expressed a similar view. However, there is another viewpoint that you might consider and that is....'

- *If you want my opinion...*
- *My advice would be...*
- *If I were you...*
- *What you should do...*
- *Think about what I said.*

As communicators, our role must be to sell at the customer's level. There is an obvious danger in instructing or lecturing the customer on how he or she should decide. Advising people might imply that you are talking down to them. A useful guideline is to use 'you' in place of 'I' whenever possible. For example, 'Don't you think it is a good idea?' sounds much better than 'I think it is a good idea.'

- *We give the service others promise.*
- *We guarantee same-day delivery.*
- *Our service is second to none.*

If you ask 1,000 salespeople what they can offer that their rivals can't they will most likely say 'outstanding service'. Phone 1,000 customers and ask what is promised by everybody but delivered by none and they will most likely say 'outstanding service'. When is the last time that you received consistently outstanding service from any company? In my discussions with buyers this was the point that most found irritating – salespeople talking about service as if they had just invented it.

'We give the service others promise' is interpreted by the customer as a slight on the opposition, of which few approve. Guarantees mean nothing unless they are spelt out and given in writing. Guaranteed by whom, for what and for how long? In fact, when customers try to establish what the guarantee is they find that it is anything but a guarantee. Buyers would like us to talk in moderate terms about our service.

- *We are cheaper.*

'Cheap' suggests inferior. 'Less expensive' implies quality at a better price.

- *I just happened to be in the area...*

Few salespeople admit to using an opening statement like this. Customers, on the other hand, say it is one of the most common of all 'openers'. The interpretation of this statement is 'I had nothing better to do with my time, so I just thought of giving you a call.' A way around this statement is to replace it with 'The purpose of my call is...'

- *We have a problem.*
- *We are experiencing some difficulties.*

It is interesting that when people hear the word 'problem' they immediately become alarmed. They see problems as requiring time and effort to resolve. However, by eliminating the word 'problem' and substituting the word 'situation' the problem is on the way to being solved.

Converting a 'problem' into a 'situation' won't make the problem go away but what it will do is change the attitudinal approach to it. Applying the same principle to our personal lives can make a world of difference.

- *As a way of compensating you...'*

For various reasons a salesperson may feel an obligation to offer the customer something extra to make up, say, for late delivery. The danger is that the customer may interpret 'compensation' as something to which he is legally entitled. This is rarely the case. There is an obvious danger in creating a precedent that every time you or your company foul up, the customer may claim compensation.

The experience of salespeople who specialise in high-revenue complaints is that if they give the customer something and emphasise that they want it to be treated 'as a measure of goodwill' the customer's reaction is generally more favourable. Perhaps the difference is that in one case he is getting what he believes he is entitled to, while on the other he is getting something that he is not entitled to and interprets it accordingly.

For similar reasons we should avoid any phrase that suggests we are judging, preaching, lecturing, criticising, blaming or advising, such as:

- *That was a stupid thing to do.*
- *What you should do is...*
- *I can't believe you could do such a stupid thing.*
- *You are wrong.*
- *What you are trying to say is...*
- *I have a better idea.*
- *Now let me give you the facts.*

Avoid also indecisive phrases:

- *Perhaps...*
- *Could be...*
- *Should be...*
- *Might be...*
- *Maybe...*

If offensive cliché-mongering on the scale just outlined is replaced with a diplomatic vocabulary, salespersons are making everyday conversational exchanges work for them. Words are never really neutral; they are often trivial and silly, but here I am demonstrating that they can be meaningful in the context of an alert mind sharpened to turn every possible occasion into a positive sales achievement.

◀ CHAPTER 5 ▶

TERRITORY AND TIME MANAGEMENT

Territory management

There are two ways to increase your sales: sell more customers or sell customers more. The key is selling productivity and time management is a critical element.

Many companies, realising the importance of cost-effectiveness, have conducted surveys on their salespeople's territory management. On average, it works out as follows:

- travel   30%
- waiting   15%
- admin, such as phone calls etc.   11%
- sales meetings   5%
- face-to-face selling   39%

If it were possible for you to increase your selling time from 39% to 52%, you would in effect be increasing your selling potential by more than 33%.

Good territory management means:

- seeing as many as possible of the right people;
- at the right time;
- under the best conditions;
- at the least possible cost;
- getting maximum sales;
- from every suitable outlet.

Salespeople see accounts as being profitable based on purchases or purchase potential. Therefore a logical starting place is to rank all your accounts based on their present and prospective order potential.

Territory analysis

Every territory will have a number of major and minor accounts along with a certain amount of new business calls that have to be conducted.

Where you have a situation in which all your calls are of equal value in terms of revenue potential, territory planning is much simpler. However, this is rarely the case.

1. Call frequency will vary from company to company. In some instances a major user may require a call every two weeks for the first three months and this must be taken into consideration when route planning.

2. Consider the time required for each call. Take the travelling time between each call into consideration.

3. Work out the number of calls that have to be made per annum.

4. It should also be possible to work out what your selling cycle is – in other words, the number of weeks or months required to get around all your customers at least once.

5. Work out the number of hours required per annum to cover all your calls.

6. Subtract the number of hours required from 1,666 selling hours and you have the actual number of hours left in which you must get in all your other selling activities – for example, canvassing for new business, reports, telephoning for appointments, time in the office and so on.

Territory management for new business

This involves dividing your territory into different sections (geographically). The idea is to concentrate on one section at a time until all

Scouring the territory will maximise selling opportunities.

prospects have been visited. You don't leave the sector at all unless you have to service an existing customer elsewhere or handle a new enquiry. By the time you reach the last sector, you will have to call back to customers in other sectors who may be ready to buy now and you will have amassed a sizeable number of new prospects.

Time management

As Arnold Bennett said:

> 'You wake up in the morning and lo! your purse is magically filled with 24 hours of the magic tissue of the universe of your life. No one can take it away from you. No one received either more or less than you receive. Waste your infinitely precious commodity as much as you will and the supply will never be withheld from you. Moreover you cannot draw on the future. Impossible to get into debt. You can only waste the passing moment. You cannot waste tomorrow; it is kept for you.'

Professional salespeople can improve sales by perfecting sales techniques and methods. Another excellent way to increase sales is to scrutinise and guard time. Only when you know what your time is worth and how to evaluate the cost of what you do is it possible to reach conclusions as to how to increase face-to-face selling time.

Managing your time effectively will increase face-to-face selling opportunities.

If you saw a colleague throw £50 of a commission payment of £200 straight into the fire, you would consider it a dreadful waste. Yet most of us will waste at least 25% of our selling time doing nonproductive things. You can waste time or kill time, or you can save it prudently and invest it wisely.

A very important guide as to how you should spend your time is the Pareto principle, called after the 19th-century Italian economist. It is often referred to as the 80/20 rule. In selling terms it means that roughly 80% of your efforts will be devoted to 20% of your sales and 80% of your sales will come from 20% of your efforts. At sales meetings, 20% of the salespeople will make 80% of the contribution. And 80% of after-sales problems will come from 20% of your customers.

Remember the 80/20 rule for selective selling. It is the policy of fishing where the 'big ones' are biting and concentrating on the activities that are likely to yield the best results.

Notorious time robbers in selling

- Bad territory management, i.e. back-tracking, hopping from one side of the city to the other.
- Lack of planning.
- No systematic approach to calls.
- Making fixed appointments where more flexible times might have been acceptable.
- Writing when a phone call will do.
- Calling when a letter or phone call will suffice.
- Spending too much time on the telephone.
- Extended lunch and coffee breaks.
- Socialising with colleagues during business hours.
- Finishing work early.
- Starting late.
- Giving sales presentations to the wrong people.

Time-saving tips

1. The first step to managing time is to identify your daily goals and priorities. Have a definite plan of action to achieve them. Organise your day in such a manner as to get maximum effectiveness.

2. Plan your work and work your plan. Some people believe that planning is merely deciding what to do in the future. However, a better definition of planning, particularly in selling, is deciding what you have to do in order to have a future.

3. Distinguish between efficiency and effectiveness. All too often we confuse them. Efficiency is doing the right job whereas effectiveness is doing the job right. Effectiveness means results.

4. Remember Parkinson's Law: 'Work expands to fill the time available.' Reduce the time available and the job will still get done.

5. Analyse the quality of your calls. Spend your time on activities or potential customers that are likely to yield the best results or are worth the task. Look for obvious time-wasters and eliminate them.

6. Write out a 'do' list and keep to it. Don't do low-priority tasks until all the high-priority tasks have been completed.

Find out where your time is spent and work with determination to eliminate time-wasting activities. Carry out the following analysis over the next 10 days. If the result is inconclusive repeat it for a further 10 days. Each block represents 15 minutes and each line seven working hours.

Time spent on these activities

Activity		Total
Time in office		
Paper work/admin.		
Meetings/training		
Talking to colleagues		
Coffee breaks		
Telephone queries		
Telephone appointments		
Telephone sales		
Telephone – personal		
Driving – travelling		
Backtracking		
Waiting on buyers		
Selling to wrong people		
Face-to-face selling		
Small talk to buyers		
Post-call activity		
Personal business		
Phoning back to office		
Other activities		
Miscellaneous		

7. Listen to self-development material in the car when travelling. Save time by training outside business hours. Keep trade magazines in your briefcase to read while waiting at reception for buyers.

8. Carry a flask and sandwiches when travelling, particularly to remote parts of your territory.

9. Where possible, handle small, marginal accounts by telephone.

10. Many salespeople sell only from 9 to 5, Monday to Friday. A reasonable number of customers are available before 9 a.m. and after 5 p.m. Every call made during these times acts as a bonus to multiply your productivity. Some customers may even be delighted to be invited to breakfast, lunch or an evening meal.

> **A good salesperson is constantly aware of new opportunities, not just between nine and five.**

Time is money

Based on a 233 working-day year at seven working hours per day, the value of your time is as illustrated on p. 90.

Looking for new business

One thing is sure. If you don't have a constant supply of live leads, you won't have any new business. Prospecting is an integral part of the salesperson's plan and must be carried out regularly to ensure there is a constant source of new contacts.

You will find leads in a variety of places but bear in mind that most other salespeople will look in the same places. If you can develop the ability to seek out business 'in parts that other salespeople can't reach', by using a creative and imaginative approach, you will improve your chances of success.

Keep your eye on the daily newspapers and business magazines for any stories of companies getting export orders, expanding their premises, taking on new staff or introducing new products. The information you gather will be useful in planning original opening statements. Note business people in the news, promotions and new appointments to senior management. If you specialise in sales to a particular market, dissect the monthly trade journals for any relevant information that may lead to orders. Get into the habit of doing this automatically, every day, not just when orders are getting thin on the ground.

If you earn (per annum):	Each hour is worth:	The loss of one hour per day over a year costs:
£	£	£
5,000	3.06	714
6,000	3.67	857
7,000	4.29	1,000
8,000	4.90	1,142
9,000	5.51	1,285
10,000	6.13	1,428
11,000	6.74	1,571
12,000	7.35	1,714
13,000	7.97	1,857
14,000	8.58	2,000
15,000	9.19	2,142
16,000	9.80	2,285
17,000	10.42	2,428
18,000	11.03	2,571
19,000	11.64	2,714
20,000	12.26	2,875
25,000	15.32	3,571
30,000	18.39	4,285

Cold canvassing

Cold calling is not the most popular aspect of selling but one that can yield profitable results. A systematic approach is necessary and there are various methods you can use.

Mailshots

Most mailshots end up in the rubbish bin without ever being read, so you have to do something different to encourage the prospect to at least see what it's about. The advantage of a mailshot is that it establishes contact with your prospect.

It must be noted, however, that the only possible way in which mailshots can be effective is if they are followed up with either a phone call or visit. Instead of going to the time and expense of a major mailshot, do a trial run of about 20 letters first. Keep your message short and be sure there is lots of 'You' appeal. Then follow them up and monitor the results to see if the exercise is worth repeating.

One salesperson writes three personal letters every day to his top prospects and follows each of them up with a telephone call. He has succeeded in increasing his success rate from 2% to 70%.

Exhibitions

These can be a tremendous source of leads and can keep you going for months afterwards. However, the floor space in a major exhibition can run into thousands of pounds before you even put your stand up. What you can do is arrange a smaller exhibition, perhaps with two other non-competitive but related businesses. The other companies' customers may become your own.

Swapping leads

Salespeople don't do this in any sort of organised fashion, but what is to stop you and your company forming an association with other, non-competitive companies to swap leads and prospects? You would be able to get all the relevant information you need about the prospect and so would be able to tailor the presentation, making it more pertinent to his needs.

Your customers

This source is all too often overlooked. Very often when we get a sale, we are reluctant to 'push our luck' by asking for referrals. Competition being what it is today, when a customer buys from you he does so for what he thinks is a very good reason. At the time he signs the order, he must feel he is making a good decision. Why not then take advantage of this by asking him for names of people who he feels may benefit from your product or service. Obviously you would never introduce this until after you have the written order in your pocket. How you ask is important. If you say 'Can you think of anybody who etc. etc.?' the response will more than likely be 'No, I can't think of anybody at the moment.' Question skilfully and make sure your customer is aware that you will use his name diplomatically and in a way that will not alter his relationship with his colleague.

Search for new business seven days a week. The very nature of our business is to be constantly aware of sales prospects. A social outing, a game of squash or a party are all opportunities to meet someone who may be a prospective buyer.

Get more out of your present customers. Nothing surpasses customer satisfaction for new business leads.

Old customer records

Look through old records periodically. A prospect who didn't buy a year ago may be in the market for your products now or in the future. Perhaps the company has a new Sales Manager or Purchasing Officer with whom you could establish contact.

Telephone canvassing

This can be very effective because it's quick and relatively inexpensive. You can establish within a short space of time whether your prospect warrants a personal call. While you may not see your prospect during cold canvassing to ascertain his potential, on the phone you may be able to find out his present supplier and how much he orders.

The telephone can also help you to:

- motivate inactive accounts;
- collect overdue accounts;
- get leads or testimonials;
- follow up mailshots or quotations;
- inform customers of impending price increases;
- check stock levels;
- maintain contact with buyers between visits.

Customer records

Paperwork can be tedious and generally you should try to cut out as much of it as possible. However, one area of paperwork is essential: the formulation of some kind of effective system for recording prospect and customer details. By keeping those records up to date, you will be able to evaluate the status of a customer or prospect at any time.

Most systems consist of a card index box with 3-inch × 5-inch cards arranged alphabetically. It's also a good idea to have a second copy of your cards arranged geographically so that if you decide to visit a particular part of the city, you have a ready list of companies. Customers and prospects should not be kept together as they require different approaches.

◀ CHAPTER 6 ▶

THE APPROACH

The importance of the approach

You never get a second chance to create a first impression. The approach, or establishing rapport, is a critical stage of the sales interview.

The salesperson has less than 60 seconds to make a positive impression on the customer. If the salesperson fails at this stage, he or she is unlikely to make a sale – in fact as many as 50% of all sales perish in the first minute.

Buyers and decision-makers are busy men. They won't waste time talking to somebody who has nothing to offer them. The customer will be as much influenced by a salesperson's appearance and manner as by his opening statement.

An original approach is a useful springboard to clinching the deal.

The most wonderful products and the most professional sales techniques will all come to nothing if you cannot get the buyer's total attention.

Avoid selling under conditions, such as a noisy workshop, that would make a presentation difficult.

If the conditions are wrong, make an alternative appointment. If you are competing with other distractions, ask the customer politely 'Could we perhaps go into your office?' Encourage the customer to talk to you in a quiet part of his premises.

Opening statements

Every customer you call on has got business problems. What you have got to do is identify the problems and explain to him in one brief opening statement how your product or service can eliminate his problems. Bear in mind that you are not selling a product or service, but a solution to these problems.

It is absolutely essential to avoid boring opening statements like:

'Good morning Mr Kelly, I represent Amalgamated Products. I happened to be passing and I thought I would give you a call.'

Or:

'Good afternoon, Mr Burgess, my name is John Brown. I don't suppose you have ever considered taking on any of our products?'

What makes these statements boring in the eyes of customers is that these salespeople are talking about themselves, their companies and their products without once indicating what they can do for the customers.

The customer is just like any other human being. He wants to talk about his company, his achievements, his problems and his needs.

There are many different types of approach you can use: examples of the most popular are given here.

News approach

Most salespeople will get a pretty good opening statement from newspaper reports or television. On occasion, a news report may centre on a customer's business: government grants, price increases, government legislation, new factories in the area, EC development grants and so on. An opening statement might read something like:

'I was reading in the newspapers this morning that the EC have granted 19 million to the western region of the country for development purposes. This is obviously going to affect your business and I would very much like to show you how my company can help you take advantage of these opportunities.'

Referral Approach

Quite a number of professional salespeople work only on recommendations from other customers. It is the most successful of all opening statements:

'Mr Shaw, I understand that we have a mutual friend in Peter O'Sullivan. He recommended that I should contact you as he believes I have something that will be of considerable interest to you.'

This approach can greatly increase your order intake by getting leads from customers who have bought from you. One word of caution: *you should never use the referral approach from leads that have been passed on by people who did not buy.* This would oviously weaken the presentation.

Bonus approach

The bonus approach is used by publishers when launching a new magazine. 'Free Holiday Competition', 'Buy This Great New Magazine Now and Get Part 2 Free!' – all these offers are 'carrots' to make us buy.

You can use a similar approach to encourage the customer to do business with you for the first time. You could say:

'Mr Pearse, my company want you to be our stockist in this area. Should you accept, you will receive a special introductory discount of 20% on all purchases.'

Remember, every customer buys for a reason. That additional 20% may be all that is necessary to encourage him to make the decision to start stocking your products.

Customer benefit approach

This is a very effective opener. It gets right down to business and creates immediate interest. Examples:

'I'm glad I caught you in, Mr Troy, I have something here I believe *you will be interested in.*'

'I know you are a very busy man, Mr Smith; however, I believe a couple of minutes of your time will prove *worthwhile and profitable to you.*'

Statements of this nature require considerable courage on the part of the salesperson. The customer will be curious but also suspicious and is likely to respond with:

'I don't believe you', 'Prove it', 'How do you make that out?', 'The only people making money are yourselves'.

It is at this point that you need to have your story ready for the customer and do exactly what he suggests – 'prove it'!

If you have sufficient confidence in your product, your company and yourself, there is absolutely no reason why you cannot use an opener like this and get straight into a successful presentation.

Curiosity approach

Assuming you have done your homework on pre-call preparation, you may have discovered a way to save a customer a great deal of time or money. This is an ideal opportunity to use the curiosity approach, which is certain to get the customer's interest.

'Mr Martin, what would you say if I told you I can save your company £45,000 a year?'

Nobody in his right mind would turn a salesperson away without finding out if the claims were true or false.

Shock approach

The shock approach appeals to one of the strongest buying motives – fear. It is used quite extensively in TV advertising. Insurance companies advertise a need for protection by showing a film of a car crash that is designed to shock the uninsured into buying.

Let's assume that you are a fire protection salesperson calling on the manager of a well stocked warehouse. Your opening statement might be:

'Mr Kelly, are you aware that insurance companies will not consider fire insurance for any premises not properly protected by fire prevention equipment?'

It may be that the customer is not aware of insurance companies' rules in this area and, being the person responsible for the premises, the statement is likely to gain his immediate interest and attention.

Service approach

Some salespeople prefer to walk into a company and introduce themselves in the hope of finding relevant information that they can use on a second visit. An opening statement might be:

> 'Mr Cullen, the purpose of my call is to introduce myself and to see if there is any way that my company can be of service to you.'

This leaves it up to the customer to explain why he has not used your company in the past, and other valuable information may be gained by the salesperson.

Finally, there is no doubt that the more opening statements a salesperson masters, the more likely it is that he will succeed in gaining an interview.

Hints on making a good first impression

1. Remember, the customer is not interested in you, your products or your company – he is merely interested in what you can do for him.

2. Some salespeople feel more comfortable offering to shake hands with the customer on the way out rather than on the way in. This is a decision entirely for each individual.

3. Don't smoke unless the customer smokes and offers you one.

4. If you wish to compliment the customer on his premises, staff or accomplishments, make sure that it is sincere. The best kind of compliment is the one that is quoted from a third party whom the customer respects and admires. However, be wary of flattery.

5. Communicate at eye level. If you are ever in the situation where your buyer is much smaller than you are or vice versa, try to manoeuvre yourself and the buyer into a position where you are communicating on the same eye level. If you have to stand, keep well back from the buyer and the difference in height will not seem so apparent.

6. Don't be a bearer of bad news. Customers will have enough problems to deal with without any additional burdens.

ACTION

Write two opening statements that apply to your product or service: one for a new business call and the second for service calls to established customers. Remember both statements should include the 'purpose of the call' and must be worded to relate to the interests of the customer.

1. _____

_____

_____

2. _____

_____

_____

The importance of product knowledge

A salesperson's credibility as an expert in his profession comes under scrutiny most when discussing or demonstrating his product. It is one of the critical areas and one which separates the amateur from the professional.

Customers rarely expect a salesperson to have committed every single technical detail to memory. There is nothing wrong with occasionally saying: 'I am sorry, I don't know the answer to that question, but I will find out for you.' This statement helps to establish the salesperson's credibility.

Product knowledge alone does not guarantee a successful sales career; however, the salesperson who establishes himself as an expert in this area will soon win the respect of the buyer and, in many cases, his order along with it. Comprehensive product knowledge covers six main areas:

1. Product features

Selling the concept behind the product is *always* as important as selling the product itself.

Every product will have many features, some of which may be unique to yours. It is important, however, that you cultivate the habit of selling the idea behind the feature. For example, not everybody in the world knows exactly what the advantage of power steering is, yet the way it is casually mentioned by some car salespeople would suggest that they do.

It is interesting to note that a simple everyday item such as a pencil will have as many as 12 features, ranging from the nontoxic paint to the material used in the rubber. The nontoxic paint will be of greater interest to a mother than it will be to a draughtsman. The material used in the rubber may be of little concern to most, but not being able to explain it just might cost you a sale.

2. Product benefits and how they relate to the customer

A survey carried out some years ago on salespeople from all over Europe indicated that only one in eight actually expressed a benefit during the sale. All others sold features.

It is your job to determine the customer's reasons for buying and, through skill and product knowledge, coordinate the product benefits with his buying motives.

Bear in mind that a benefit must:

(a) solve a customer problem;
(b) save time or money;
(c) increase productivity or profits;
(d) decrease costs or overheads;
(e) improve image or prestige;
(f) satisfy a particular customer need.

While there will be other obscure benefits, most of them will be covered under these headings.

3. Product performance

In some respects this category of product knowledge is the most important. If the salesperson can't demonstrate how it will solve the customer's problems, satisfy his demands or fulfil his needs, it is unlikely that he will make a sale.

Many salespeople can explain how their product meets general needs. However, the professional goes one step further and demonstrates how the product is going to satisfy the customer's specific requirements.

4. Product price and how it compares with the competition

Invariably price objections are raised by customers when they do not perceive the product's value. So in order to sell the product's value we must have the product knowledge. This means that the salesperson, when faced with the objection that his goods are more expensive, must be able to substantiate that his product is worth the extra money. On the other hand, when faced with the reverse problem – that his products must be inferior because they are cheaper – he has to prove through product knowledge that the quality he claims does, in fact, exist.

5. Product construction

As the customer and the product designer are unlikely to meet, the only way that the buyer can understand how the product is put together is through the salesperson. What materials are used, how it is assembled, and how it is transported is valuable information. An increase in the cost of raw materials may eventually find its way to the selling price of your product. When this is explained to the customer, he may accept a higher price more readily.

Apart from background knowledge of the manufacturing process, you must be able to explain the firm's service, distribution and credit policy. A total understanding of the company's procedure for granting credit helps to explain credit terms. A knowledge of shipping procedures might help to explain why a customer has to wait an extra week for delivery.

The salesperson's ability to explain the terms, the limits of what is and what is not covered under warranty, can be most important in making sales. A very high number of service calls and customer complaints come about because products are used incorrectly. In many cases these could have been avoided by a little extra explanation by the salesperson.

6. The present state of the industry

Practically every type of business is covered by several trade magazines. Salespeople should keep themselves up to date with what is happening in the industry. This serves a useful purpose in explaining market trends, forecasts and new ideas and gives a valuable advantage over competitors.

Knowledge of your competitors is as important as any other branch of product knowledge, because if you don't understand the competition, you are indirectly helping them. You must minimise your weaknesses while offsetting the strengths of your rivals.

Every company claims to have at least one unique selling point (USP). It is this unique point which must be highlighted against the selling points of your competitors.

Customers rarely buy without 'shopping around' to some degree and your knowedge adds a valuable dimension to the sales story. The story, like any other, sounds much more convincing when it is being told by an expert.

Finally, the acquisition, application and regular updating of product knowledge are tremendous confidence-builders for the salesperson, not only in meeting objections but also in his attempts to command the customer's respect. The professional salesperson knows that there is no substitute for knowledge because nothing can hide ignorance.

A. Write down the 'unique selling points' of your product or service. Get into the habit of highlighting them during your sales presentation.

ACTION

1. _____

2. _____

3. _____

4. _____

5. _____

6. _____

7. _____

8. _____

9. _____

10. _____

B. Get into the habit of stressing and personalising the benefits to each individual customer of your product's features. They should be related as follows:

One of the features of this product/service is _____

_____

_____

This enables you to *or* the advantage is _____

_____

_____

Which means to you _____

_____

_____

C. Remember, customers are not interested in features. They buy benefits. To increase your awareness of the importance of stressing benefits carry out the following exercise and review it constantly.

Features	Advantages	Benefits to the buyer

Pre-call preparation

All professionals must prepare before they tackle a job. A barrister will have all the relevant facts before he enters the courtroom. A surgeon, before he makes the first incision, must know exactly what he is doing and what he is trying to achieve. Can you imagine the results if these professionals tried to do their jobs without preparation and knowledge?

The professional salesperson must also do his groundwork. The immediate results are increased self-confidence, since confidence comes from knowledge, and a more effective presentation. But obviously the major benefit is more orders – more quickly.

The more information you gather about the person and the company you are going to visit the better prepared you will be.

The prospect

You will need to know the prospect's name, first name as well as surname. Make sure you have the correct pronunciation, particularly if the name is unusual. Find out his title and, very important, whether he has the authority to make the final purchasing decision. Some background information about the person may be very useful – has he been in the company long, where did he work before? Perhaps you have some common interests or hobbies. From your telephone call could you assess what type of person he is? Does he seem approachable and open to new ideas or products? Could you assess what buying motives will appeal to him? Record all this information on a customer profile card for future reference.

The company

What nature of business is the company involved in and what products do they have on the market? Find out the size of the company and the number of people employed. The names of the receptionist and the general manager will prove helpful. Does the company have any branch offices or associations with other organisations? Who are their competitors and is there anything special about the company you should know? Is there a market for your products in any other department within the organisation? Finally, make sure the company has a good credit rating – there's no point in selling goods if you have to wait an unreasonable length of time for payment.

Your preparation

Establish what competitive company they are presently dealing with. You should know as much as possible about your competitor's products and service already. What advantages do your products have? Find out how much your prospect orders and how often.

Analyse exactly what you are trying to achieve by your call. Obviously you are trying to make a sale, but make sure you are selling the right product in the right quantity. What problems can you help the customer to solve by introducing your products? Will you save him time, money, space? Remember, this is much more important than the actual product itself. Why should he deal with your company as opposed to his present supplier? The answers to these questions are vital to your presentation.

Remember the steps of the sale are *attention, interest, conviction, desire* and *action*, so think about each stage of the sale. What will your opening statement be? It must be interesting enough to *gain attention*. How will you *maintain interest*? Can you use some third-party stories that are relevant to his business? What exactly will you do to *secure conviction* and

Remember the steps of the sale are: attention, interest, conviction, desire and action.

establish desire? If you have dealt with a similar company before, use your experience to assess what objections are likely to be raised. Ensure that you have a good response to any problem area. Finally, consider what closing techniques you can use to *get action.*

Customers appreciate professional preparation because few sales people do it!

Amazingly, many salespeople enter the customer's office without basic sales aids and company information. Before your visit, check your briefcase. Have all your brochures and samples in a place where you will find them easily. It's most unprofessional if you have to start rooting through a packed briefcase to get them. Make sure you have a current price list, order forms, bank drafts, leasing forms and so on. Finally, check your appearance and don't forget to have an ample supply of business cards.

Talking to the right MAN

There is an expression used in selling: 'Contact the MAN – the person with Money, Authority and Need. We have all made the mistake of giving superb presentations, only to be told 'This looks pretty good – I'll have a chat with my boss when he gets back on Friday.'

We do have the right to ask a customer if he has the authority to buy. Any mature human being will appreciate that you, as a business person, do not wish to waste their valuable time or yours by giving long-winded presentations without the possibility of a decision.

There are many ways you can get over this. Try one of the following:

'Mr Cairns, are you the person who will be making the final decision on this?'

'Will you be making the decision on your own or should we invite somebody else into the discussion?'

'Assuming that my proposal is acceptable, Mr Cairns, will you be signing the order?'

An efficient salesperson really should find out before approaching the contact whether or not he is the one who is going to make the buying decision.

How much do you know about your average customer? Select one of your customer record cards at random and answer as many of the following questions as you can. On completion of the exercise, calculate the points you have scored. (Grades given below.)

	YES	NO
Do you know? …		
The customer's full name (spelling and pronunciation)	☐	☐
Full title (managing director, sales manager, etc.)	☐	☐
His/her background?	☐	☐
Length of time with his/her present company?	☐	☐
His/her interests and hobbies?	☐	☐
The receptionist's name?	☐	☐
Porter/security guard's name?	☐	☐
General manager/chief executive's name?	☐	☐
Customer's assistant's name?	☐	☐
The customer's company's full range of products?	☐	☐
The customer's competitors in the market?	☐	☐
The company's origin?	☐	☐
Whether they have branch offices or associate companies?	☐	☐
Number of employees in the company?	☐	☐
Which of your rival companies he/she also deals with?	☐	☐
The best time of the day to call?	☐	☐
His/her motives for buying your product?	☐	☐
What 'unique selling points' would be of benefit to him/her?	☐	☐
What experience he/she has had with your rivals?	☐	☐

Score 10 points for every 'yes' answer. You score as follows:

150–200   Excellent.
120–150   Good, but could be improved.
90–120   Average. Probably reflected in the sales results.
50–90   Below average. Weak relationship with this customer.
0–50   Very poor. Do you really care about this customer?

Handling comments and questions about the competition

It is rare for a customer to make a purchase without having checked out the competition. Invariably you will be confronted with questions, comparisons or objections raised by the customer. Some important points to bear in mind (and practise constantly) are as follows:

1. Don't put down or advertise your rivals

The golden rule of selling is 'never knock the competition', whether in a crude way, such as:

'Never heard of them.'

'I never knock the competition – *no matter how bad it is.*'

or in more subtle ones.

Some time ago my colleague responded to a telephone enquiry, signed up a lucrative contract and on leaving asked the customer where he got our name. The customer responded: 'from one of your rivals'. We would not have got the order if our rival had not mentioned it. Why he singled us out we will never know but I will be happy if he continues to do so.

When a competitor is mentioned, pay polite attention and say something like: 'very nice people' or 'I know the company' or 'yes, I've heard of them'. By making such comments you are acknowledging their existence without committing yourself one way or the other. Why give free advertising, particularly to your competitors?

2. Watch your body language

When the competition is mentioned by a buyer it is understandable that the salesperson may interpret it as a threat to getting the order and become physically agitated.

Without wanting to, it is easy to become defensive and the customer thinks: 'I wonder why he is so worried about them? Maybe I should check them out.'

It takes a lot of training and self-discipline to cope with competition on an unemotional basis. Buyers are professionals and some quite deliberately observe the salesperson's reaction when competitors are introduced into the discussion. Anticipate that a rival's name will be brought up and practise your response.

3. The customer says the competition knocked your company

It would be quite understandable if you over-reacted to a suggestion from the customer that a rival was making 'wild accusations' about your company. If and when this happens don't fall into the trap of replying with:

'The things I could tell you about that crowd!' or

'People in glass houses shouldn't throw stones.'

While the reaction may be understandable, it is professionally unaccept-able and likely to work against you.

Some years ago, on a joint call with a professional salesperson, I saw an identical situation being turned to an order-winning advantage. The conversation went as follows:

Customer:	'Your rivals claim that you have not been around long enough to be able to give the service that is required. What have you to say about that?'
Salesperson:	'Well, first of all I am pleased to hear it, Mr Smith. If my rivals are singling me out for special criticism the only interpretation I can put on it is that I am beginning to worry them. Would that be a fair interpretation?'
Customer:	'Yes, I suppose that's a reasonable conclusion.'
Salesperson:	'In a backhanded, indirect manner our rivals singled us out in a complimentary way for "special mention" and I can't give you a better reason to buy from me.'

The customer bought.

4. Keep the trading standards up

From personal experience and customer comments it is easy to categorise rivals as top-class or poor. Some salespeople dwell too much on making comparisons between their own companies and the bad ones. Usually this is a mistake, because it encourages the customer to perceive the overall standard in your industry as poor. The reason: the salespeople told him. Tell him how good *you are*, not how bad the others are.

Some years ago I wanted to purchase a product for our training centre. I saw two different salespeople and had difficulty in deciding on the product that best fulfilled my requirements. The following day I received a phone call from one of the salespeople and explained that I had not, as yet, made a decision, as I had two proposals to look over. He enquired who the other company was and I responded with something like: 'Is it really important for you to know?' He said: 'Well, you have to be careful because there are a lot of "cowboys" in our business.' Not only did he not get the order but my perception of him and his industry went down.

5. Don't single out a competitor

As an inexperienced salesman and out of respect for my rivals (which was the first thing I learned about selling) I went to the other extreme. To demonstrate my lack of fear of the competition, when a rival's name came up I would say: 'Oh yes, we are very familiar with them. In fact they are our arch rivals.'

Having lost a number of orders I began to ask myself why they were giving orders to salespeople who, at the time of my interview, had not spoken to the customers. It took me too long to realise that I was giving the customer vital competitive information which was undermining my sales pitch. Ever since then I handled the question differently by stating:

> 'Mr Smith, we have 27 other companies competing with us in the market place. All are taking a share of the market because they are all pretty good companies.'

By answering in this way, I am improving or maintaining the customer's perception of the industry. Furthermore, I hope the customer is saying to himself: 'I haven't got time to look at 27 other companies. This doesn't look too risky and if this guy makes it easy for me to buy, I might as well get this out of the way and get on to something else.'

◀ CHAPTER 7 ▶

THE SALES PRESENTATION

The Presentation

At some time during the selling process you will have to make a sales presentation. In many cases it is not possible to carry the products to the customer, so the sales presentation must be designed to highlight the features and benefits of the product. Regardless of whether you are demonstrating an actual product or making a presentation through brochures, samples or specially designed material, the objective will be to convince the buyer that:

1. the need exists;

2. your product can satisfy that need;

3. he can afford the purchase.

The effectiveness of a sales presentation is measured not in how well you present, but in how well the buyer understands and is motivated to buy. The best way to present your product is to ensure that it satisfies six basic requirements:

Plan
Pattern
Power
Proof

Pictures
Participation

Plan

Good presentations don't just happen, they are planned. And as you prepare your presentation you should incorporate into it the customer's details you have compiled.

Only the relevant materials relating to this buyer should be included. Personalising or tailor-making the sales story to the customer's requirements will show that your sales message is unique to his needs.

Pattern

The presentation must follow a step-by-step logical sequence that will guide the customer towards a mental acceptance of the product.

In all instances, the target of your efforts is to provide the customer with logical and relevant information. A good rule is to present only what relates to his expressed needs.

Power

The power behind the presentation is a combination of enthusiasm, planning, self-confidence and a positive mental attitude. Enthusiasm, so often referred to as the method that persuades people without pressurising them, must be injected into the discussion. Remember that, no matter how many times you have told your story before, the customer is only hearing it for the first time.

Proof

It is not sufficient for a salesperson simply to state that his machine produces quality or that there is a saving of so much per year. Whenever possible, give proof of all such claims being made about your product. Most customers have doubts or reservations about the claims made by salespeople. A third-party letter from a happy user is more credible in the eyes of the buyer than the verbal claims of the salesperson.

Pictures

We are a visually oriented society. We grow up surrounded by the influences of television, advertising, and all kinds of visual stimuli.

Visuals help the salesperson control the presentation and maintain the customer's attention. They force the salesperson to organise his thoughts in an orderly fashion and condense the message into a concise and more understandable story.

When relying on the spoken word alone to communicate, an estimated 90% of a message is misinterpreted or forgotten completely. We retain only 10% of what we hear. Adding appropriate visual aids to the spoken word increases retention to approximately 50%. No words can equal the power of a picture and sales aids help us to communicate more effectively with the buyer.

Participation

Getting the customer in on the act is very important. He should be involved with action and words. Observe his reaction to elements of your presentation and ask plenty of questions to ensure that he is with you all the way. Any negative comments should be handled to the buyer's satisfaction before continuing.

Your presentation is designed to provoke reaction so watch carefully for signals.

We all like to think that our opinions are important, so when a customer makes a positive remark, stop and ask why this particular point is of interest to him. Listen carefully to the response; he is about to give you a very good reason as to why he should buy your product.

Buying signals

When the prospective buyer begins to take an obvious interest in the presentation, which will be indicated by his actions, remarks or response, it generally means only one of three things:

1. He has seen or heard something that he can apply to a particular need.

2. He is interested but has not yet decided to make a purchase.

3. He has already made the mental decision to buy.

The customer will indicate this interest either verbally or non-verbally. Some of the non-verbal clues are:

- picking up the product and reading the instructions;
- going back to an item you have already shown him;
- eyes dwelling constantly on a particular item;

- moving forward to get closer to the product;
- suddenly sitting up in the middle of the presentation.

The verbal clues come in the form of questions or statements; for example:

- 'What kind of guarantee do you give with your products?'
- 'Do I have to pay cash right away?'
- 'Do you have quantity discounts?'
- 'What colours do you have it in?'
- 'How much is it going to cost?'
- 'How much space will it require?'
- 'Do I have to pay for supplies?'
- 'Can we take this on lease?'
- 'Do you have a maintenance contract?'

Buying motives

Every time we buy something, we do so because it satisfies a need or desire. When we are expressing the benefits of our product to the customer, we must appeal to his dominant motive for buying. These motives and needs can only be discovered by asking problem-seeking questions like 'Where do you see a need for change in your present system?'

Having discovered the customer's problem areas we can give him added reasons for buying by tying product benefit in with his buying motives. Buying motives fall into two groups, emotional and rational:

Emotional reasons for buying are:

fear	of competition, of being left behind
envy	of others' successful achievements
vanity	recognition by others of having made a wise decision
love	approval of colleagues, family and friends
entertainment	enjoyment, relaxation and so on
sentiment	family tradition, local company
pride	being associated with a successful project
pleasure	derived from the appearance of the new purchasing, design, etc.

Rational reasons for buying are:

profit	increased efficiency, less wastage
health	less hazardous to heart, less strain
security	well established firm, brand names, proven track record
utility	easier to use, less effort, time-saving, etc.
caution	fewer service calls, durable, long life, and so on

It is quite possible for a customer to buy for many particular reasons. In fact a couple buying their first home may buy for every one of the emotional and rational motives. It is therefore very important to understand what motivates the customer to buy your products.

When a customer asks questions that indicate interest it is a tremendous opportunity to close the sale. For example:

Customer:	'Can we take this on lease?'
Salesperson:	'Yes, Mr Kelly, you may. I can arrange either two years or five years. Which would suit you best?'

Some salespeople miss this opportunity by giving a simple 'yes' response, without following up with a closing statement.

Selling the idea behind the product

In the selling process, the product is only of secondary importance. The primary factor is the idea behind the product, the purpose that the product fulfils.

We don't sell calculators, we sell speed, accuracy and efficiency. We don't sell education, we sell career success and personal development. What ideas do you sell?

The salesperson's role is less difficult when a clear understanding of selling ideas is accepted. Charles Revson of Revlon Cosmetics put it in a nutshell when he said: 'In the factory we manufacture cosmetics and in the pharmacy we sell hope.'

Remember, customers buy ideas first.

The customer's mental buying process

Herbert Casson said: 'The buyer's mind is the raw material out of which sales are manufactured.'

113

Remember that the professional salesperson's definition of a sale is the exchange of a product, idea or service to the mutual benefit of buyer or seller.

A sale is made in the mind of the buyer: therefore it is essential to establish an understanding of the customer's mental buying process and plan your sales story simultaneously along the same logical pattern.

As you progress through your sales presentation, the buyer is saying in his own mind:

I am important.
Consider my needs.
How will your ideas help me?
What are the facts?
What are the snags?
What will I do?
I approve.

You must have a clear understanding of what happens in the buyer's mind from the initial approach right up to the close of the sale. You must see this as an organised logical process that must be carried out if the order is to be obtained.

Emotional influences in the sales presentation

It is easy to fool ourselves into believing that because we sell top products for top companies it follows that we should get the business. The question is, however, how many of our customers make logical decisions?

Some years ago, Harvard Business School carried out research with the US top buyers to uncover what proportion of a buying decision was based on emotion and how much on logic. It came up with this staggering result: 84% of all buying decisions are based on emotion!

While it may be difficult to accept these findings, it may help to examine the complexity of decisions taken in the private life of the average consumer. The most important decision a person will make is to marry, a decision that indisputably has its origins in emotion. How much of the purchase of the wedding day attire has been influenced by emotional motivation? Would it apply as much to the acquisition of cufflinks and jewellery as it would to a pair of knickers? If the decisions were based on logic nothing more than the proverbial fig leaf would be required in the marriage ceremony and even less on the honeymoon!

While the decision to buy clothes may have begun as a logical need, the final decision to purchase that garment was motivated by a number of emotional motivators, such as colour and design. Take the average buyer who is making these emotional decisions in his or her personal life and put them behind a desk – do they suddenly start making logical decisions? The answer is no – they will continue to be influenced by their emotions.

Throughout my career I have known people to change jobs for a better car or a bigger title but less money. If monetary logic had prevailed they wouldn't have moved.

If it is accepted that customers are influenced by their emotions, then it can be accepted that the customer's emotional attitude will influence the chances of getting the order.

Four major areas of influence will be:

- the customer's attitude to you, the salesperson;
- your company's treatment of the customer in the past;
- price and credit policy;
- the customer's relationship with his present supplier.

Addressing these points to the satisfaction of the buyer will help in closing successful sales. The buyer must also be satisfied on a number of other issues. In the advertising world they are referred to as *Rascil* factors and they also form the major characteristics of a good advertisement:

*R*eputation of your company (when established)
*A*uthorised products and services (brand names, trade certs.)
*S*afety factors (money-back guarantees, etc.)
*C*ompleteness of service
*I*ntegrity of staff
*L*ocation and areas served.

Communicate to the customer that the company scores high in all these areas and there is a good chance of achieving a sale.

Hints on making effective presentations

Keep it short and sweet
Mark Twain listened attentively to a speaker making an appeal on

Once you have caught the customer's attention, you must maintain it.

behalf of a charitable cause. Thinking the charity to be worthy, he determined to donate $100. The speaker droned on monotonously. Twain's initial enthusiasm was gradually squandered. When the speaker finished, Twain went up to him, handed him one dollar and told him he had talked himself out of $99. Moral: say as little as necessary to communicate your message!

Tell a stimulating sales story
A story sounds more convincing when told by an expert who conveys the point with enthusiasm. Memorise vital points of your presentation and tell only those parts which are relevant to each individual customer.

Avoid emphasis on technical features
A technical explanation is usually unwarranted and difficult to understand. The buyer won't always be the user, so explaining how to clear a paper jam on a copier may be totally irrelevant and a waste of valuable selling time.

Some time ago I was doing role plays with twelve experienced salespeople from the business equipment world. At the end the following points were clearly evident:

1. Each demonstration took, on average, 36 minutes. How many busy buyers are likely to be stimulated by a sales presentation lasting that long?

2. Of the 22 features demonstrated, none was converted by anybody into a corresponding benefit.

3. Of the features mentioned, only three were relevant to the buyer, but attention was not drawn to them.

4. Nobody mentioned that the features were unique, which they were!

5. Salespeople occasionally brought up product weaknesses, referring to what the product would not do rather than what it would – for example, 'this machine does not have a reduction facility'.

Remember, the buyer is interested only in what the product or service will do for him or her, so stressing only the relevant benefits are a must.

On the other hand, the buyer may be familiar with the technicalities of the product, so try to discover quickly the extent of his or her knowledge. Let them ask questions if they so desire but get back to benefits as quickly as possible.

Emphasise unique selling points

Not enough salespeople take the trouble to find out the 'unique selling points' of their company, service or product. Even fewer actually mention it during a sales presentation. It is your biggest competitive edge and it is your job to point it out to the customer.

In order to express with confidence the fact that the product or service has unique aspects, it is important to have a thorough knowledge of the advantages and disadvantages of competitive products and services.

Remember, buyers need justification for making a purchase and if the unique selling point is consistent with the buyer's need, a sale has a better chance of succeeding.

Use 'you' appeal throughout. Think of your presentation from the customer's viewpoint – in other words: 'What's in it for me?'

Explain guarantees

Guarantees are frequently abused by salespeople, but used properly they can be a powerful sales aid. Few customers receive a detailed explanation of what protection they can expect. It is only when something goes wrong with the product and the customer is in a highly charged frame of mind that he discovers what is not covered. Here are two good reasons why guarantees should be explained:

1. The risk involved in making a purchase is greatly reduced in the buyer's mind by money-back, replacement or parts-and-labour guarantees. If your product or service is supported by built-in buyer protection it is important to highlight it, otherwise a valuable sales opportunity may be lost.

2. In the event of after-sales problems with the product, needless irritation will have been avoided.

While this point has been covered under 'phrases to avoid', above, there is no harm in repeating it because of its importance – avoid 'verbal guarantees', such as:

'We guarantee same day service.'

'We guarantee four-hour response time to service calls.'

The salesperson's credibility should never be brought into question at any time. When a customer challenges the salesperson to explain the 'verbal guarantee', it invariably transpires that 'guarantee' is only a 'declaration' of what the company would hope to achieve under 'normal' circumstances. Some time ago I witnessed the following exchange between buyer and seller:

Seller: '... and, of course, we guarantee a response time of four hours in this area.'

Buyer: 'And what happens if it is five hours before you get here?'

Seller: 'Our service manager will be very pleased if you bring that to his attention; he will be most anxious to put that right.'

Buyer: 'But you suggested a moment ago that this situation would never arise – you just guaranteed four hours.'

Seller: 'I see what you mean, Mr Smith, and I would be a fool to suggest that we never get it wrong. In fact, last Christmas the roads were so bad it was three days before we got to some of our customers.'

Buyer: 'So what you are really saying is that if the roads are OK, if none of your engineers are laid up, if their cars don't break down, if all your customers don't require service at the same time and if we phone in at the proper time, you will guarantee four-hour service?'

The salesperson was embarrassed and it was only his skill and experience that allowed the conversation to continue. The only requirement was a gracious apology. He learned a valuable lesson and now speaks in more moderate terms about his 'guarantees'.

Create a more relaxed selling atmosphere
Selling isn't telling. It's all about asking questions – the right questions. No matter how enthusiastic you are about your product or service, or how entertaining or exciting your proposition may be, customers will eventually switch off to one-way communication.

Fundamental to top-class professionals is the ability to communicate with customers in a relaxed manner. A tense, nervous salesperson can put the customer on edge and is not conducive to a positive selling atmosphere.

It is understandable a salesperson will experience some apprehension when approaching a buyer for the first time but it will get a little easier with experience. If you develop to the stage where you don't feel tension, you are either a remarkably calm person or not demonstrating the respect the buyer deserves.

One of the first questions I ask people going into selling it: 'What are the attributes of a successful salesperson?' The following are typical of the responses:

'You've got to have the gift of the gab.'

'You must have the ability to talk somebody into buying something that they don't really want.'

'You have got to develop a good "sales spiel".'

With such poor perception of selling, one wonders why they select it as a profession. Not one buyer I questioned was aware of a salesperson who succeeded on the basis of the projection of these unprofessional attributes. On the contrary, professional selling has nothing to do with a 'gift', developing the 'spiel' or pushing products on people who don't need them.

When I first went into selling I was led to believe selling was about being pushy and verbally persuasive. The result was that I projected the image of the 'typical' salesperson. Like so many people at that time, training was given only by the top companies and most people had to learn the 'hard way'.

After a number of weeks and few sales (the job was commission only), I reflected on the comments that people had made when they *didn't* buy to see if I could uncover why I was not selling. The most consistent comment that I had heard was: 'It's too expensive.'

Could it be my lack of experience, or was I doing something wrong? But then I thought it couldn't be me because several people had told me I was a great salesman.

Doubts set in and self-analysis began. If I was such a 'great salesman' how come I was not getting many sales? It suddenly dawned that contrary to being a 'great' salesperson, I was a poor one. It was a lesson I was never to forget and from that moment on I changed my entire attitude to what selling was all about. Instead of telling, I started asking questions. Sales began to improve – dramatically. I was still making embarrassing mistakes, but at least I was beginning to do something right. So the moral of the story is: if you hear people telling you that you are a 'great salesperson', it's not a compliment, it's an insult.

What can be learned from this experience is the importance of developing a selling style that is totally devoid of any unnecessary pressure. A good salesperson will monopolise the listening, not the talking. The buyer can become actively involved in the discussion only when he or she is answering questions. Consider this small piece of wisdom:

> The wise old owl sat on the oak.
> The more he heard the less he spoke.
> The less he spoke, the more he heard.
> Why not be like that wise old bird?

One of the best ways of relaxing the customer is to get him talking about things that he feels comfortable with; for example:

'What made you go into this business in the first place?'

'You have been successful in your profession; may I ask you to what you attribute that success?'

'Your company have a good reputation in the market-place. What do you do that others don't?'

Buyers, like all of us, enjoy talking about their successes. One word of caution, however: if the buyer has the slightest impression that these questions are just a technique or that you are trying to flatter him or her, it may well backfire on you. The personality skills in being a stimulating conversationalist are based on a genuine interest in others. Listening forms a major part of exchanges and Rudyard Kipling had his own way of teaching us this art:

> I keep six honest serving men,
> They taught me all I knew;
> Their names are What and Why and When
> And How and Where and Who.

Think of the sales made to date in your career and I believe you will agree that the common factor with all your buyers is that you created and developed a relaxed business relationship. Is this coincidence?

There are many ways to learn the skills of the successful salesperson:

1. We can learn from personal experience, often referred to as the 'school of hard knocks'.

2. We can learn from the experience – the successes and failures – of others.

3. We can have intensive training by the experts in our profession – the customers.

4. We can combine all the experiences – our own, others' and our customers'.

The most painless way of acquiring skill and knowledge is having the facts from every source and using them to your advantage. Consider this quotation from Chesterfield:

> There are three classes of people in the world. The first learn from their own experience – these are wise; the second learn from the experience of others – these are the happy; the third learn neither from their own experience nor the experience of others – these are fools.

The successful salesperson will constantly appraise his or her failings against the experiences and views of others – particularly the customer. The attitude should be to eliminate the negatives and accentuate the positives.

20 major reasons for failing – according to buyers

According to buyers, a salesperson fails if he:

1. Knocks the competition, own company or colleagues.

2. Has an embarrassing lack of self-confidence.

3. Does not come to the point quickly enough (beating around the bush).

4. Overstays his welcome.

5. Gives the impression that he knows it all.

6. Talks too much and asks too little (boring)

7. Knows little about the product, service or competitors.

8. Pounces back with clever clichés and reacts badly to the buyer's opinion.

9. Appears to be interested only in selling the product.

10. Exaggerates the benefits of the product or service.

11. Gives poor overall presentation.

12. Talks about his own interests.

13. Knows nothing about the buyer's needs.

14. Has no enthusiasm for his job.

15. Interrupts the buyer, and is over-anxious to get his point in.

16. Whines about poor business.

17. Has a poor personal appearance.

18. Puts too much pressure on the customer to buy.

19. Makes no attempt to close the sale.

20. Tries too hard to impress.

One thing is certain, without the ability to get inside the customer's head, it is unlikely any reasonable measure of success will be achieved. It is not part of the customers' role to rehabilitate salespeople who constantly switch them off. Their contempt for a particular salesperson may be expressed with objections such as: 'I'm too busy at the moment'; 'We are happy with our present supplier'; or 'Your product is too expensive.' These may be genuine objections but customers are unlikely to tell a salesperson, 'I don't like you or your manner, please leave and don't come back!' They will protest by *not* buying or leaving it up to the salesperson to decide what went wrong.

How many times have you walked into a store and felt pressure to buy or felt so annoyed at the standard of service that you walked out? How many people voice disapproval to the offending salesperson? Very few! The people we call on are no different. They won't tell you how they feel about you but they will tell you how they feel about other salespeople.

If you take the major reasons for failing listed above you will notice they fit into one category – attitude. It is important to recognise that an attitudinal change is required and for this mental alteration to take place, three things must happen:

1. There must be a sincere recognition that a change is required and the areas involved must be clearly identified. In other words, if you don't know what the problem is, there is no point in trying to find a solution.

2. You must be passionately interested in this change taking place and your emotions must be aroused by the prospect of the benefits to be gained.

3. You must set out with determination to alter the offending habits. Recognise that attitudes and habits tend to go together – change one and you automatically change the other.

Use good third-party testimonials

Someone has said that the buyers of the world are divided into two categories: leaders and followers. If you can find a way of communicating the positive views of some of your product's users who are also known to a prospective buyer, you have given the proof that may be necessary to clinch the sale. If the TV viewer perceives that Daley Thompson likes Lucozade, he is led to believe that it must be good for him too.

If you have a good relationship with a happy user, ask for a letter recommending your product. When the appropriate moment arrives, make sure the prospective buyer sees it.

In the absence of written proof, use available character sources, such as newspaper cuttings, trade references and so on. If you are quoting a happy user, be sure that your quotation is accurate. Otherwise use an expression such as 'I believe this to be true'.

Sell the sizzle, not the steak

People don't buy products, they buy what the product will do for them. In other words, they buy the end result. For example:

People don't buy:	*... they buy:*
furniture	comfort, style
cars	transport, status
TVs	entertainment
insurance	protection, security, investment

Too much emphasis is placed on features by salespeople and customers do not always see the immediately corresponding benefit.

Use words that sell

There are many definitions of selling. One that sums it up adequately is: 'assisting prospective buyers to arrive at a decision that will be of benefit to them'. The world is full of people who have difficulty making up their minds – particularly where money is concerned. It is a good idea to make the emotional transition from presentation to sale as painless as possible for the buyer, so it is inadvisable to use words or phrases that scare, such as:

'Contract'	This suggests legal implications. (Use 'agreement')
'Signature'	Nobody likes signing. (Let's get rid of the paperwork)
'Cost'	'Valued at' or 'worth' sounds more appealing.

Write down all the words you use during the presentation and consider what other interpretation can be made. If there is another word which conveys the same meaning in a more positive light, start using it.

Sales presentation – self-appraisal

Rate your performance under the following headings.

(5) Excellent (4) Above average (3) Average (2) Below average
(1) Poor

1. Standards of presentation material? ☐

2. Ability to use the material professionally? ☐

3. Ability to personalise the presentation? ☐

4. Ability to use the six Ps – plan, pattern, etc.? ☐

5. Ability to recognise buying signals? ☐

6. Knowledge of buying motives? ☐

7. Ability to sell the idea behind the products? ☐

8. Knowledge of customer's mental buying process? ☐

9. Knowledge and use of your USPs? ☐

10. Ability to relax the buyer? ☐

11. How do you score on 'buyers'' reasons for failing? ☐

12. Ability to be different? ☐

13. Use of third-party references and testimonials? ☐

14. Use of sales literature and visuals? ☐

15. Degree of company knowledge (your own)? ☐

16. Degree of company knowledge (customer's)? ☐

17. Degree of competitive knowledge? ☐

18. Degree of product knowledge? ☐

19. Degree of industry knowledge? ☐

20. Ability to organise your thoughts properly? ☐

Total ☐

Score as follows:

20+	Poor
40+	Below average
60+	Average
80+	Above standard to excellent
100	Excellent

Using sales literature and visuals

Research has indicated that 97% of all information is communicated to the brain through the eye. Therefore, the more the customer sees, the greater the chance he has of remembering it. Unfortunately, few salespeople take the time to develop their selling material, resulting in a confusing presentation. Generally, the use of sales aids by salespeople fall into three separate groups:

1. Salespeople who are not supplied with presentation material and who, instead of designing their own, rely too heavily on the product's brochures to sell. Furthermore, most brochures are designed for reading close-up and are not conducive to two-way communication, making the sales discussion difficult to follow.

2. Salespeople who are supplied with sales presentation kits and who are in my experience rarely trained in their proper use and even more rarely monitored.

3. Salespeople who utilise visuals to their best advantage, by personalising them for their particular market, achieve a significant competitive edge. Customers do appreciate salespeople putting in that extra effort on their behalf. It also demonstrates a level of commitment to the customer's needs.

It is known from tests carried out in the USA by Dr Walter Scott that if 1,000 people were handed an advertisement for a company's products, this is what would happen:

1 day later	25% would have forgotten
2 days later	50% would have forgotten
4 days later	85% would have forgotten
7 days later	97% would have forgotten

If this information is correct, there are two vital points to be learned. First, the sale must be closed when the salient points are uppermost in the buyer's mind because one week later, he will have forgotten all the benefits exalted during the interview. Second and more importantly, what chance has a customer of remembering the details of a verbal presentation?

Some hints on using visual aids

1. Remember the presentation folder is for your use and not the customer's.

2. No matter how many times you have told a story or shown a particular visual, the prospect is hearing it for the first time. So be enthusiastic.

3. Keep your visuals clean. A shabby visual will communicate all the wrong things. It is blatantly unprofessional.

4. Become totally familiar with your visuals. In many cases you may have to talk about them while they are the wrong way up in relation to you.

5. Avoid showing two pages at the same time. If you are demonstrating a point from an open folder, cover one of the pages with a plain white sheet of paper. This ensures that the prospect is focusing on the factors you consider vital.

6. Avoid the customer getting hold of your folder, because by doing so you have lost control. In the event of it happening unavoidably, stop talking and redirect the customer back to a point that you wish to make. At the same time politely take back the folder.

7. Show the absolute minimum required to convey your message.

8. Don't read. Use different words to make your point. This will help to reinforce it.

9. Personalise whenever possible. There is always the temptation to use a 'general sales patter'. Your presentation will be greatly improved if you tailor your words to convey that you are showing these visuals because they apply to the customer's situation.

10. Show only what is required. There is rarely a need to show everything in the presentation kit.

11. Verify understanding. Don't continue unless the customer has completely understood. A good snappy presentation will maintain his interest. There is nothing to be gained by emphasising a point the prospect has grasped already.

12. Arrange your visuals before you meet the prospect. Fumbling

around will distract the customer's attention.

13. Properly used the presentation is a powerful persuader. It provides the opporunity of eliminating objections before they arise.

14. It is very difficult to make a sale solely on the basis of a conversation. What we say is more believable if it is backed up by visual proof.

15. With time, energy and a little imagination, it is possible to develop a highly professional, stimulating presentation.

◀ CHAPTER 8 ▶

MAKING APPOINTMENTS AND SELLING BY TELEPHONE

Making Appointments

There are definite pros and cons in making appointments to see prospects. With cold calling, you may cover a large territory quite quickly but may yield a low number of live leads. Telephone appointments, on the other hand, must be carefully planned so as to avoid racing from one side of the city to the other.

Ideally you should avoid making fixed appointments except in cases where you are sure to be on time. A number of customers will agree to an approximate appointment time, e.g. late morning or early afternoon. This arrangement gives much needed flexibility to the salesperson's day and eliminates the pressure we have all experienced at one time or another: 'Should I stay here in the hope of getting a sale or should I leave to be on time for my next appointment?'

Probably the best compromise is to make at least two *firm* appointments per day – one first thing in the morning and the other first thing in the afternoon. The rest of the day can be used for flexible appointments, where a fixed time was not specified, or for cold canvassing.

There are special techniques to be used when ringing up for appointments. Many salespeople find it difficult to make a good snappy presentation on the telephone through lack of eye contact and body language which act as pointers to their progress. It is imperative not to give too much away to the prospect, so avoid the temptation of trying to sell on the phone. Basically you want to give him just enough information to make him interested in seeing what you have to offer.

Put yourself in his shoes: he has no idea that you are going to contact him. You must convince him that your visit will be short and that your proposition is interesting enough to warrant a hearing. You don't have very long to achieve this so you must sound as businesslike and professional as possible.

Pre-plan your approach

Set the objective of the call. Obviously you want to make an appointment, at a suitable time for *you*, so what times and alternatives will you offer the prospect? Have your diary in front of you all the time. Do you want to visit him or invite him to your showrooms or to an exhibition? Be absolutely clear in what you are trying to achieve. Anticipate his objections to seeing you and pre-plan your response.

You are not trying to make a sale, so your objective should be to:

gain his *attention* with a crisp businesslike opening;

get him *interested* by telling him your ideas can help him;

close the appointment by offering alternatives.

Or, to put it in a nutshell: *ring up*, *fix up*, then *hang up*.

Dealing with reception and secretaries

Decision-makers are busy people and it is not possible for them to see everybody who requests an appointment. They will talk only to the salesperson who promises to offer something special. It is for this reason that many of them will have their calls screened by their secretaries. While secretaries rarely influence the decision to buy, they can make it extremely difficult for you to speak to or see the decision-maker. It would be unwise not to recognise the importance of their role. Find out their names and treat them with respect. Be pleasant and polite without being false or overpowering. Regardless of their manner or attitude, never become rude or indignant. When seeking their help in getting an appointment, use golden phrases like:

'What is your opinion?'

'Can you use your influence?'

'I'd like your advice.'

Suggestions for getting past reception

When the receptionist answers, your attitude and voice should convey firmness but in a friendly manner. For example:

'Good morning, would you please tell your Managing Director, Peter Smith, that Michael Farrell is on the line for him? Thank you.'

There is an air of finality about this type of statement that does not invite any further questions from the receptionist.

In general, at this stage, one of four things will happen:

1. You will be put through directly to your contact, so be prepared.
2. You will be told he is not available. Just say 'Thank you, I'll phone again.'
3. You will be put through to his secretary. In this case, you should repeat your introductory approach.
4. You will be asked the purpose of your call by either the receptionist or secretary.

When this happens say politely:

'It's about a letter I sent him,' if indeed you have sent a letter.

'I want his advice on a new idea – he is expecting my call.'

'I have some interesting information for him.'

'I have been asked to contact him.' (If challenged to say by whom, say your MD.)

'Well, it's rather complicated and I would really much prefer to talk to him directly about it.'

'Yes, I would be delighted to tell you the details – however, I would prefer Mr Smith to instruct me to do so; can you put me through to him, please?'

Prepared customer responses are a vital element of handling objections.

If you still fail to get through to your contact, don't waste time discussing any of the details of your proposal. Simply ask the secretary if she can make an appointment on your behalf. If this is not possible avoid a lengthy discussion and tell her you will phone back at a later date.

On being put through to your contact

There is the crucial point of the telephone call. This is where appointments are gained or lost. A confident approach comes from knowing exactly what you plan to say and how you propose to handle his objections to giving an appointment.

The systematic application of a plan will soon become automatic.

It is very important to develop your own telephone approach and great time and care should be devoted to it. Write a script for alternative openers. While you may feel a little uncomfortable initially, after a few calls you will begin to feel much more at ease. Plan each stage of the telephone interview and what statements you propose to use.

A standard introduction is a five-step process; for example:

1. 'Good morning, Mr Smith.'

2. 'Thank you for taking my call.'

3. 'Do you have a few moments to talk to me?'

4. 'My name is Michael, Michael Farrell from Amalgamated Products.'

5. 'I am sure you are very busy so I will come straight to the point.'

This must be followed by a real 'interest-getter'; for example:

> 'Mr Smith, like all successful business people you are interested in any idea that will increase sales or profits.' (You should now pause for a response from the customer.) 'My company have introduced some exciting new ideas that have proved very successful with your fellow professionals. I am calling to ask for a few minutes of your time to demonstrate how these ideas can help increase your profits. Are you in the office most of the time, or should I make an appointment?'

It is important to note that the following sequence of customer objections to appointments comprises only examples of the most common type and the salesperson would not necessarily encounter all these objections in the space of one call.

Customer:	'Can you send me some details in the post?'
Salesperson:	'Yes, Mr Smith, I can send you plenty of literature. However, the ideas I'd like to discuss with you are new and best explained when applied to precise information. That's why it needs a brief two-way discussion. How are you fixed on Friday at 10.40, or would a little later suit you better?'
Customer:	'Look, I'm just not interested at the moment.'
Salesperson:	'Mr Smith, I have yet to talk to customers who *were* interested initially. However, what they were interested in was the increased profits resulting from implementing these ideas. Any idea that saves your company money is worth investigating, wouldn't you agree?' (Pause for response.) 'Can I see you on Friday morning as I suggested or will later in the day be more suitable?'
Customer:	'No, Friday's out, I'm just too busy at the moment.'
Salesperson:	'Mr Smith, I appreciate the pressures that are on your time. However, I believe you and your company will benefit from our discussions and I would like the opportunity to show you how we can save your company money. Our discussion will take no more than about eight minutes. At that stage, if you still feel that I have nothing to offer, I will leave, agreed?'
Customer:	'It's a bad time of the year really. Our budget is spent.'
Salesperson:	'Mr Smith, the purpose of my wanting to meet you is to see whether we have something to offer you now or in the future. In any event, I can promise you your time will not be wasted. Do any of the times I suggested suit you or would you prefer next Tuesday morning?'
Customer:	'I'm trying to save money, not spend it.'
Salesperson:	'Yes, Mr Smith, I think I know how you feel about it. In these days of rising costs and high interest rates, we have all got to be careful how we spend our money. However, may I put an idea to you?' (Pause for response.) 'If you were completely satisfied that I could actually save you money, would you talk to me?'

	(Pause.) 'OK: when can we get together? As Friday is out, would Monday afternoon suit you or would you prefer Tuesday morning?'
Customer:	'Look, I'll get back on to you. What's your number?'
Salesperson:	'It is kind of you to suggest it, Mr Smith. However, as I spend most of my time on territory, I'm rarely in the office. Could I recommend that we make an appointment for Monday at 2.30 and if for any reason you are not available perhaps you would be kind enough to get your secretary to phone the office and change the appointment?'
Customer:	'All right, Monday at 2.30 will be fine.'

One essential rule in making appointments by phone is to offer alternative times when making the request for an appointment. However, use your discretion – don't be too overpowering. Similarly, every answered objection should be followed up with either a request for an appointment or a question. The purpose of asking the question is to control the discussion.

When you have achieved your objective, confirm the appointment, thank the customer for his time and politely terminate the call. Record the details of the conversation on your prospect card and enter the appointment into your diary.

If you fail to get an appointment, it is essential to leave the door open for another call in the future. Your attitude on terminating the call must be professional and businesslike. An example of this is:

Salesperson:	'Mr Smith, obviously we are not going to do business on this occasion; however, it was very good of you to give me so much of your time. I will be in your area sometime in the near future and I will drop in some details. Perhaps we will get the opportunity of meeting? In the meantime, I hope you have a very successful year.'

The 10 steps of the telephone interview

1. Greet the customer.

2. Thank him for taking your call.

3. Ask him for a few moments of his time.

4. Introduce yourself and your company.

5. Give an opening statement and identify the purpose of your call.

6. Ask for the appointment and offer alternative times.

7. Anticipate the objections.

8. Overcome the objections.

9. Ask again for the appointment.

10. Close the interview.

Selling by telephone

Recently, a number of international businessmen were asked 'What do you fear more than death?' They replied 'Making a speech.' If the same question were put to salespeople, I believe their reply would be 'Using the telephone.'

Few sales tools enable a salesperson to save or organise time for greater efficiency than the telephone. Yet so many are inhibited by an innate fear of it. Fear that they will be unable to project their personality, that the customer will say 'no', or refuse to give them a hearing. Why should salespeople feel so intimidated by an instrument that they had little difficulty in using throughout their teenage years, running up high phone bills to the annoyance of their parents?

Remember – the telephone is an instrument for your convenience, not torture!

Driving a car into the city is a traumatic experience for anybody learning to drive and this analogy also applies to selling by telephone: the more you do it, the better you become.

Let us look at some of the ways in which the telephone can be used in selling:

Making	appointments
	cold calls
Following up	quotations
	mailshots

	sales enquiries
	a letter
	leads
	exhibitions and trade shows
Getting	repeat orders
	'referrals'
	market information
	'add-ons' to the order
Increasing	sales orders
Dealing with	low-potential accounts
	complaints
	overdue accounts
	service problems
	customer queries

Like every other tool, the telephone has many limitations and it will never adequately replace face-to-face communication. It would be unwise to try to sell highly technical products by phone, yet much of the pre-call planning could be done in advance of your visit. Any salesperson wishing to maximise selling efficiency must master the art of telephone selling. Having all the other skills such as handling objections and closing the sale are a distinct advantage – skills that come naturally to all top salespeople. All that is required is a formula for the telephone sale, as summarised below.

Techniques for selling by telephone

Preparation and planning
- Have all relevant information at your fingertips:
  - sales aids
  - price lists
  - brochures
  - market information
  - competitive information.

Call plan
- Decide who you are going to phone.

- What is the objective of the call?
- Decide on opening statement.
- Write down points to be made in logical order.
- Anticipate objections.
- Decide on alternative closing methods.
- Concentrate for two minutes on your call.

Introduction
- Identify yourself and your company.
- Ask for your contact and check pronunciation.
- When put through, explain purpose of call.
- Ask the customer for his time.

Fact-finding
- Ask questions – why, what, where, when, how, who?
- Get the customer to talk about his business.
- Write down useful information.
- Lead the conversation and question skilfully.
- Identify the customer's problems.

Discuss and agree customer needs
- Explain your understanding of customer problems.
- Back up claims with good third-party stories.
- Get enthusiastic about your proposals.
- Convince the customer that *YOU* believe in what you are saying.

Sell your product
- Create customer desire to buy.
- Sell the related benefits.
- Explain how your product can help the customer.
- Do not mumble the price to the customer.
- Sell your product with energy and enthusiasm.

Overcome objections
- Listen to the objection.
- Restate the objection as a question.
- Ask for agreement about your interpretation.
- Seek agreement.

(See next chapter for more on these points.)

Close the sale
- Ask for the order.
- Do not give up on the first 'no'.
- Persevere pleasantly
- Restate benefits if necessary.

(See Chapter 10 for more on these points.)

After the order is given
- Thank the customer for his order.
- Reassure him of his wise decision.
- Leave him on a happy note.
- Thank him for his time.
- Let the customer hang up first.

Check your ability to use the telephone. Using copies of this chart fill one in now and further ones periodically over the next six weeks. Alternatively, you may prefer to ask a colleague or manager to fill one in for you.

Using the telephone – assessment sheet

Description	Poor	Fair	Good	V.good	Excellent	
Telephone personality						
Preparation for calls						
Voice projection						
Telephone empathy						
Attitude						
Opening statements						
Projecting enthusiasm						
Professional approach						
Gaining attention						
Getting information						
Making the sale						
Handling objections						
Closing the sale						
Handling complaints						
Handling accounts						
Making appointments						
Effective listening						
Human relations						
Telephone confidence						

Remarks _____

_____

_____

_____

◄ CHAPTER 9 ►

OVERCOMING OBJECTIONS

To the professional salesperson, meeting objections is a time of excitement and high drama. They know that good customer objections are milestones towards the sale, not obstacles or brick walls with 'no sale' written across them.

A sale does not begin until the customer starts to object, and an order obtained without an element of customer resistance is extremely rare. Good objections are healthy – they inspire communication and are as vital to salespeople as a rudder is to a boat.

Objections will occur at any time during the sale. They are very often indications that the customer is interested. Some buyers will prefer not to show their hand until all the negatives are eliminated. Generally speaking, the customer who has no questions to ask has no desire to buy either.

Reasons for objections

No attempt is made here to review every possible reason as to why objections arise. The intent is to focus on some of the most common causes of sales resistance, and having created that awareness, eliminate as many as possible.

Firstly, it is important to mention one of the major causes of customer resistance to being sold and that is the attitude of the salesperson. Ask any buyer to list the reasons he does not buy from certain salespeople and he is likely to tell you that he objects when the salesperson:

- Reacts badly to his opinions, questions or objections.
- Makes exaggerated claims about his product or service.
- Insists on doing all the talking and no listening.
- Appears to know little about his product.
- Gives the impression that he knows it all.
- Bounces back with a smart response to every question.
- Embarrasses him by scoring victories with technical knowledge.
- Disregards his needs, his fears or his feelings.

Your role, at the best of times, is difficult enough without making life any harder. It is important to analyse your performance to ensure that the customer's reasons for not buying were not attributable to you or your attitude.

The importance of self-analysis is reflected in the knowledge that, even if your attitude and behaviour is exemplary, you still have to deal with customers who, for one reason or another, have a genuine resistance to buying.

Responding to objections

1. Listen carefully to the objection
It is imperative to listen, with *all* your senses. The buyer's opinion is important to him and you must show that it is also important to you by hanging on to every word. Listening includes good eye contact and nodding your head to suggest understanding; both of which enhance the selling atmosphere.

2. Remain calm
Give the impression that, whatever his fears may be, you are quietly confident that you can resolve them. You must be careful that your body language is not communicating agitation or annoyance. Remember the buyer is subconsciously influenced by your attitude and manner.

3. Never interrupt
Apart from it being very discourteous, you may as well say 'shut up, what I've got to say is much more important.' When the customer has finished, pause briefly and consider his question.

4. Restate the objection phrased as a question
By doing so you are ensuring that you are not misinterpreting the

customer's message; it gives you valuable time to think of an acceptable response; and it demonstrates to the customer that you don't have a 'pat' answer.

5. Use a consistent tone of voice
It is essential to talk in a consistent manner and tone throughout the presentation. Lowering the tone of your voice will suggest defeat and raising it will convey antagonism.

6. Empathise with the customer when responding
There is nothing more frustrating than expressing an opinion that is not really accepted. The old idea of answering objections with 'I see what you mean all right, but ...' is not only a direct contradiction, but also infuriating. Your response must show consideration for the customer's point of view. Remember you can never change a man's opinion once you have challenged his judgement.

7. Seek the customer's agreement from your response
Every time an objection is raised it is essential that the response is agreed by the customer before continuing. The technique is to finish your response to the objection with a question that is logically answered in the affirmative.

Handling price objections

Many salespeople try to sell on price alone. Usually this is a mistake because price is little more than a reflection of the product value. If price were the only consideration in the minds of customers, there would be no Mercedes cars and no Chanel perfume, or thousands of other prestige products. Buyers invariably look at more than just the price factor.

At some stage during the presentation you must be prepared to demonstrate how the price of the product can be justified. Therefore the key to handling price during the sale is to have a definite plan of action. Introduce price in such a way that the buyer can see it in its true perspective as one of a number of factors and not necessarily *the* deciding factor.

Convince the customer your product is invaluable to him *before* mentioning the price.

In understanding price we must analyse the products that we sell. Are they price-positive or price-negative? Generally it can be stated that what the buyer *desires* or *wants* is price-positive and what he *needs* is price-negative. The telephone bill for £150.00 will seem more expensive than the video recorder he wants at £1,000.00. A bill for £200.00 for green fees will seem much more expensive than a set of golf clubs costing many times that amount. You may buy a car for £15,000.00 but the insurance bill for £1,000.00 will seem outrageous.

Where customers need certain products, the only time that price will play an insignificant role is when the customer has an urgent need or the product is in short supply. During the fuel crisis of the mid-seventies people went to extreme lengths to get petrol at any price. The more closely the product matches the customer's predominant motive for buying, the less expensive it will appear to him. If you can prove that your product represents real value for money, it is unlikely that price will be an insurmountable obstacle.

Your attitude to price is also very important. If you believe your product is expensive, you will influence the customer to think in the same way.

Hints on handling price

When the customer says that the product is 'too expensive', establish exactly what he means by that. It can mean any one of a number of things, from what he paid before to what the competition is charging or what he believes it should cost. Bear in mind that price in many cases is the smokescreen for the underlying objection and only through clarifying the objection can we discover whether it is sincere or false.

When customers say that your competitors have similar, less expensive products than yours, work out the cost difference and show the customer what additional benefits he is receiving for his 'extra' money. For example, if the difference is £100, you merely have to justify the customer spending an extra hundred, not the entire cost of your product.

A high-priced product does not seem quite so expensive when compared favourably with another item that is higher in price. Similarly, it is important to gather information about the performance, durability and acceptability of higher- and lower-priced items. In so doing, your product can be compared against the long-term benefits of your competitors.

Emphasise *value* for money, not price alone.

Sell, emphasise and stress the value of the product – make the benefits outweigh the price. The size of the price tag will be minimised or exaggerated in the eyes of the customer depending on how you emphasise the benefits.

There are two schools of thought on explaining price. Some salespeople prefer to give the customer all the bad news at once, working on the principle that the price 'problem' can only get better.

Other salespeople prefer to break the price down into manageable amounts. Instead of quoting £1,000.00 for an order of 10,000 units, they will quote the price as 10p per unit. Another technique is to show how much the items cost in terms of time. If you are selling a desk and chair that cost £2,000.00, you might say that the furniture has a guaranteed life span of 10 years, which works out at £16.67 per month. Supermarkets use a similar technique by saying '75p per quarter' rather than '£3.00 per pound'.

Techniques for meeting objections

There are definite techniques to help overcome objections. They are as follows:

The forestalling method

The method of anticipating a major objection and bringing it up yourself is an excellent technique, because the buyer doesn't feel that he has to defend his point of view.

Salesperson: 'Mr Keller, I realise that you may feel this is something that would appeal only to manufacturing companies; however, I would like to show you how this will be of particular benefit to you.'

The digging technique

At any time during the presentation the customer may object. It is essential to ensure that you are not wasting time answering the wrong objection. In order to uncover the hidden resistance use probing questions like:

'Well, apart from price, Mr O'Neill, is there anything else that would stop you from going ahead with this?'

If the customer implies that this is his only objection, you should logically only have to answer that objection and you have a sale. On the other hand, if he does have another objection, answer that one first. This is probably the source of his biggest resistance.

The defer technique

The time when salespeople are faced with some of their most difficult objections is at the start of the presentation. One way to overcome them is to use the defer technique, which is probably the most underutilised skill in selling. It is very effective when you are faced with initial objections.

Another time at which the defer technique is particularly effective is when the inevitable price question is brought up by the customer. Most salespeople try to avoid introducing the price until the customer has had an opportunity to appreciate the value of the proposition. This is a skill in itself, as the customer will be suspicious if you keep refusing to tell him.

Customer: 'Look, before you go any further, what's the price?'

Salesperson: 'Mr Roberts, I realise that you are anxious to know what this is going to cost; however, may I ask you to leave that area until we have discussed what your particular needs are. At that stage I will be in a position to give you all the information you require. Is that OK?'

You will find that this statement is rarely challenged.

The boomerang method

This is where a question or the objection is thrust back on to a customer.

Customer: '£2,000 is too much to pay for a word-processor. I am sure I could get one cheaper than that.'

Salesperson: 'Mr Keegan, I realise that there are a lot of other word-processors on the market and of course a number of them are less expensive than this one. However, based on our discussions, it appears that this one is best suited to your needs. And in relation to cheaper models, wouldn't you agree that nothing is cheap if it doesn't meet your requirements?'

145

The indirect denial

In this technique you agree with the customer and go on to sell the product's main benefits:

Customer: 'This product is very expensive.'

Salesperson: 'Yes, Mr Hayes; of course, being such a reliable model, it will not require costly service and repairs like most other models, and that must be an important consideration, wouldn't you agree?'

The superior point technique

This is the technique of offsetting a major point against a minor one – to minimise a real objection by pointing out an offsetting advantage:

Customer: 'If we get this new carpet we will have to buy new wallpaper for the lounge.'

Salesperson: 'Mrs Watson, this high-quality carpet will last a lifetime. If you wait until you are changing your wallpaper in two years' time, this carpet will certainly cost you more then than it will now.'

Arming yourself with a variety of techniques will help you quash objections.

Finally, it is essential to have available as many responses to objections as possible. If you are getting the same type of objections every time, there is always the possibility that your sales presentation is weak in some areas. The reasons should be identified and eliminated.

Write in your own words how you would answer these fairly common objections:

Customer objection: 'We are happy enough with our present suppliers.'

Your response: _____

_____

_____

Customer objection: 'Thank you for coming in to see me. Will you put your proposal in writing to me? As soon as I have had a chance to look at it, I will get back to you.'

Your response: ————————————————————————

————————————————————————————————————

————————————————————————————————————

Customer objection: 'I need more time to think about this.'

Your response: ————————————————————————

————————————————————————————————————

————————————————————————————————————

◀ CHAPTER 10 ▶

CLOSING THE SALE

Every phase of the selling process has unique aspects, but none is as significant or as critical as the close. For every salesperson this is the moment of truth.

When you decide to close the sale, you have already done 90% of the work. But it is the final 10% that you get paid for.

As the Sales Manager of any organisation will verify, the only way a salesperson's performance can be measured is by the consistent production of orders. A salesperson who cannot close is not a salesperson but a mere conversationalist.

While it is true to say that many sales are lost long before the order is asked for, failure to follow the presentation with a good strong closing sequence can result in that order going to the first person who can.

The basic principle behind the use of effective closing techniques is: when sales are plentiful we need these skills to take advantage of the opportunities that prevail; when times get tough and the competition gets keener, we need the very same professional techniques to survive.

Inside the customer's mind

Before a sale is completed, it is imperative to empathise with the customer and consider what is going through his mind at this particular moment. He may never have seen you before and may never see you again. He is now being asked to part with money for a solution to a problem he may not have been aware of until you walked into his office.

Bear in mind that your rivals are faced with the very same obstacle.

The salesperson who, through a creative presentation, can eliminate most of the customer's fears before attempting to close the sale is most likely to succeed.

Before buying, the customer must be satisfied that:

1. You are a professional, you represent a professional organisation and everything you have told him is truthful and above reproach.

2. The product or service you are selling has a successful track record and will do all the things for him that you promised it would do.

3. He completely understands exactly what he is receiving for his money and, just as important, what he is not getting.

4. In the event of any post-sale problems you and your company will honour your commitments without any further investment of time or money on his part.

5. All questions have been answered and there are no other problems to stop him from buying except the decision itself.

The salesperson who observes these crucial points and makes the effort to build them into the presentation will find closing sales much easier.

Points to remember on closing the sale

First-time stories are best. No sales presentation sounds as good the second time around. Close when all the benefits are fresh in the buyer's mind. There is an old rule in selling: the order that is within reach today will be over the hill tomorrow.

No matter how great the temptation, never beg the customer to buy. On the rare occasion that this method succeeds, you lose credibility and any prospective repeat business.

Customers are unconsciously affected by your attitude. Radiate confidence, by your manner, posture and voice, that his order is inevitable. A most important factor in closing sales is the positive expectation by the salesperson that he is going to sell.

Watch out for buying signals. If none is forthcoming, ask the customer how he feels about the colour, size, quantity or delivery dates.

Get the customer to say 'yes' as often as possible during the

Bring techniques previously learned into play to help close the sale.

demonstration. This encourages a positive response when the order is asked for.

When asking for the order be polite, persistent and pleasant. An aggressive or presumptuous manner suits few and is offensive to most. At the same time it is imperative that you demonstrate a quiet calmness that dispels any idea that survival depends on getting this order or that getting an order is a unique experience.

There is no such thing as a single psychological moment to close. Avoid falling into the trap of assuming that the opportunity to clinch the sale has passed. Remember the ABC of selling: Always Be Closing.

Don't throw in the towel after the first 'No'. It may mean that the order has been asked for too early and the customer requires more information before deciding. The secret of great closers is they always try one more time to close the sale.

Never introduce something into the close that has not been discussed earlier. This will divert the customer's attention away from the most critical part of your presentation.

When the order has been asked for, say absolutely nothing. He who speaks first is lost. We read in the Bible about how Samson slew 10,000 Philistines with the jawbone of an ass. That same weapon is being used by salespeople all over the world to lose orders every day.

While a little humour is encouraged in the sales demonstration, beware of clowning around at the closing stage. The danger is that the entire presentation becomes a joke and the customer is let off the hook.

No matter how receptive customers may be to your proposition, they will nearly always need a 'push'. The extent of the 'push' should be dictated by the extent of the resistance.

Avoid questions that invite a negative response, for example: 'You wouldn't care to have it, would you?' or 'I suppose you wouldn't be interested.' This approach is most unlikely to inspire the customer to buy.

Try to keep something in reserve. Many experienced salespeople hold back one major point of their sales presentation so that if the customer says 'no', they can introduce a final 'carrot' and clinch the sale.

Dealing with call-backs

The importance of getting the order the first time is reflected in the knowledge that call-backs are never as productive as they promise to be. Customers invariably remember the price tag only and the desire to buy recedes. The buyer who is 90% sold today may not even talk to you tomorrow.

It is true, of course, that no matter how good you are at closing the sale, there will be times when the buyer will not be able to make a decision. The mark of the true professional is the person who leaves the door open to try another day. It is a combination of experience and perception that tells you when to politely terminate the interview and leave without the order.

In the unavoidable event of a call-back, avoid starting the conversation with a question like 'Have you thought it over?' In practically every case you will find that the response is negative. It is far better to say 'A very important point that I forgot to mention to you last week was....' This gives you the opportunity to reopen the discussion and close the sale.

n closing one sale lways leave the ay clear for the ext one.

Techniques for closing the sale

The suggestion close

On the occasion when the buyer requires a little gentle persuasion a suggestion along the following lines may be all that is required:

> 'Mr Maloney, may I suggest that we tie up the paperwork now and, rather than take up any more of your time, I will talk to your Stores Manager and agree a delivery date.'

The assumption close

The customer's manner, body language or comments may indicate to you that the decision to buy has already been made. Use expressions like 'When you receive your machine', 'How do you wish to pay for this?', 'Where will we install it?' The customer answering any of the questions in the affirmative is giving you the signal to write up the order.

The assumption technique means not having to ask the customer a direct question about the purchase. This gives him the chance to make a painless decision.

Alternative close

This is probably the most popular technique of all. The idea is to offer two options to the customer in such a way that the buyer chooses between two positive alternatives.

- 'Would you prefer to pay cash or should I invoice you?'
- 'Do you want delivery today or will next Tuesday do?'
- 'Will I put you down for 20 or would it be safer to take 25?'

In general, the customer responds either by selecting one of the options or by saying 'I haven't decided that I want to buy it yet.' In which case, try to find out what it is that is holding him back.

The isolation technique

This close is highly effective and applies to all types of selling in which the customer has the opportunity to choose from a large selection of products. Rather than confusing the customer with the entire range, the salesperson, having assessed the buyer's needs, selects three of the items that most suit his requirements. The salesperson then proceeds to eliminate, with the customer's agreement, the least attractive proposition. By following the same process, he then eliminates the next item by explaining why it is the less attractive of the two remaining, isolating the only remaining option.

The active close

This is a particularly effective technique and to be used when the customer's reaction appears to be neutral. The idea is to ask a question and to follow it up with an appropriate movement. A business equipment salesperson may say 'Could you show me where you wish to have this machine installed?' At the same time the salesperson rises from the chair, followed, in many cases, by the customer. Once the buyer starts discussing where he wants his machine installed, the sale is made.

The concession sale

Every product on the market will be sold on the basis that the product or the company possesses one 'unique selling point'. This may be in the form of payment terms, free after-sales service for six months, money-back guarantee, special introductory offer or perhaps a combination of 'carrots'. These are all designed to induce the customer to buy.

The technique is to keep something up your sleeve and produce it only when it is going to make the biggest impact. It may well be that the biggest stumbling block to the sale is one of the concessions you are at liberty to make. Remember that the close is the time that the customer is making up his mind and anything that will help him decide favourably must be used at that point.

The balance-sheet close

There is nothing preventing any salesperson from using every imaginable close on one customer. That is why a salesperson requires all the techniques that he can get. The balance sheet is an effective method of closing not only because it gets the buyer involved, but also because it highlights the reasons why the decision to buy is the right one.

Draw a line down the centre of a page and on one side write the reasons 'for', while on the other side the customer writes down the reasons 'against'. If you are doing your job right, the reasons 'for' should outweigh completely the reasons 'against'. Major advantages of this type of close are that it gives you the opportunity of restating the benefits and it forces the customer to bring all his objections out in the open.

Part-by part technique

Often customers have grave difficulties making major decisions, perhaps because the price appears to outweigh the benefits. The part-by-part close is an effective means of overcoming this problem.

Instead of asking the customer to make a major overall decision, break it down into parts. Car salespeople, in particular, have an advantage with this type of close: they get the customer to agree on each feature of the car, e.g. the colour of the upholstery, the sun roof, the car stereo and so on. When the salesperson gets agreement on each point the decision to buy has already been made.

The urgency or impending event close

It is a strange trait of our nature that while we may have to think about a proposition that will be profitable to us, we cannot resist the fear of losing out on a special offer.

Essentially, in this technique you urge the customer to act immediately rather than putting off the buying decision. It is extremely effective, but obviously should only be used when you have something special to offer. For example:

'Mr Hill, we have decided to introduce a special offer for one week only. If you sign the order today, I will include the latest executive swing chair with your new desk.'

'Mr McMillan, this product will have a 17% price increase next week. You were planning to reorder your stationery soon anyway, so will I process your order now?'

Narrative close

This close consists of telling the customer a story that relates specifically to his business and how your product helped an associate or successful businessman. In our profession we will meet many customers who follow the examples of other people in their business. The purpose of this technique is to encourage the buyer to see himself as having made a wise purchase – just like his associates.

> 'Mr Leonard, I have a letter here from one of your business colleagues. He has been using our filing system for the past three months. Like yourself, he was concerned that ... but as you can see, he is more than happy with the system and the problems that it has solved for him.'

The 'if' technique

There will be occasions where the customer will not respond favourably to the close. He may feel that he is being pressurised into making a decision. The chances are that he will respond by saying 'I want to think it over.'

The salesperson can divert the customer from his last comment by saying something like:

> 'Mr O'Neill, if you do decide to take this investment policy, over how many years would you want to take it?'

The customer can be brought back into the presentation by the salesperson asking logical questions. After a short time the customer may have forgotten his original objection and the salesperson can make a second attempt at the close.

From what you have just read, write three closing techniques and personalise them to your own business.

1. The suggestion close _____

_____

_____

2. The urgency or impending event close ————————

    ————————————————————————————

    ————————————————————————————

3. Draw up your side of the balance sheet close:

Salesperson's reasons for	Buyer's reasons against

CHAPTER 11

LEARNING FROM THE EXPERIENCE OF OTHERS

Failures need not be written off as total losses: the lessons learned can become the foundations on which success is built. There are few successful salespeople in the world who will go through their careers without fouling up at some time. It stands to reason that if we can avoid some of the more common failures, success must be a little easier to achieve.

Salespeople's reasons for failure

Admit failure is possible, but *learn* from it.

There are many ways to learn the skills of the successful salesperson. Let us call on those who have experienced failure and recovered to tell the tale. Every acknowledged failure experience is an important education for those wishing to succeed in selling. These were the comments of some salespeople about their own failures:

- 'I believed that my way was the only "right" way.'
- 'After 15 years I thought I had nothing left to learn.'
- 'I didn't listen to the criticisms and views of others.'
- 'I spent too much time planning tomorrow and forgetting today.'
- 'I blamed everybody else when sales were down.'
- 'I fooled myself that I was putting in the effort.'
- 'I spent too much time and energy working out why something couldn't be done.'
- 'I believed that nobody wanted to see me before 10 a.m.'
- 'I was just another salesperson, no different from the rest.'
- 'No clear direction or specific goals to achieve.'

- 'I didn't use my day properly.'
- 'I neglected my customers too long.'
- 'I didn't appreciate the importance of pre-planning.'
- 'I believed that price was *the* deciding factor.'
- 'I got too friendly with customers, then found it hard to sell.'
- 'I was too subservient, becoming a slave to everybody.'
- 'I was too influenced by negative remarks from others.'
- 'I hadn't the confidence to ask for an order.'
- 'I didn't look or act like a professional.'
- 'I tried too hard to be liked by people.'
- 'I was too concerned about my rivals.'

Management reasons for sales failure

Management give their own reasons for the failures of sales staff. When managers were asked for the main reasons for salespeople's nonperformance, these were given:

- lack of effort;
- failure to follow sales policy;
- fear of the competition;
- ineffective use of time;
- lack of imagination;
- putting things on the long finger;
- little or no planning;
- a defeatist attitude;
- fear of the buyer;
- no interest in sales development.

An important aspect of the development of salespeople is the constant appraisal of their overall performance. If one can eliminate all the red flag areas, then success is nearer realisation. When sales are down it is a good idea to check yourself against the reasons for failure.

Eliminating failure and taking stock of the customers' viewpoint is an absolute must for the true professional.

A. Write down five important aspects of selling that you have learned through your own experience.

1. _____

2. _____

3. _____

4. _____

5. _____

B. Read back over the two lists of reasons for sales failure. There are 31 in all. Score 10 points for every one that presently applies to you. Grades are as follows:

0–20	Excellent.
30–70	Now that you know what they are – eliminate them.
80–130	You may have faults but honesty is not one of them.
140–190	Now you can see where some of your sales have gone.
200–250	This will require a big change of attitude.
260–310	Aren't you glad you bought this book?

Other factors contributing to failure

It goes without saying that the morale and motivation of salespeople is of prime importance. Without it few salespeople will get inside the door, let alone get the chance to close a sale. All of us are eventually influenced by continuous negatives: here are some that should be avoided like the plague.

Associating with negative people and listening to their views

The last thing we need is people telling us that the job is harder than we already perceive it to be. We just might begin to believe them. When and if, through their influence, they have reduced your earnings, will they make a contribution to your mortgage repayments?

Newspapers, radio and TV reports

The media thrive on sensationalism and bad news. You would have to be inhuman not to be saddened or depressed by some of our daily news stories. Even if they don't affect you they may affect others. Bringing up bad news in a sales situation is nothing short of suicide. It may be part of your job to be well informed and if you are not affected by the news, that's fine; but keep it to yourself. In any event it is probably wise not to listen to or read news until the evening, when it doesn't affect your motivation.

Some years ago I accompanied a salesperson to one of our prospective customers who was leaving that day on his summer holidays. He was in radiant mood and I believe that he would have bought from anybody that day – well, nearly anybody. For reasons best known to the salesperson, he said 'Wasn't that a dreadful tragedy this morning!' and proceeded to further dampen the customer's spirits with all the horrific details. I watched in astonishment as the prospective sale slipped further away. We didn't get the order – owing, no doubt to the flagging morale of the customer, caused entirely by the insensitivity of the salesperson. The moral? Keep the bad news to yourself.

Home life

Our domestic lives have a bearing on our ability to perform well at work. Most salespeople have two businesses to run: their personal and their working lives. The importance of striking a balance is reflected in the fact that if you pay too much attention to one the other will suffer until both become difficult to handle. It is a delicate operation to strike an acceptable balance. If you find that improvements can be made, then make them. Being conscious of it is all that is required.

The effects of worry

More people die from the effects of worry than from any other known disease. Personal problems and worries about health, finance or family will eventually eat into the hard-earned morale of even the most successful salespeople. Worry has its own 'vicious circle'. Start worrying and motivation takes a dive, which in turn affects enthusiasm, resulting in a drop in sales. When you stop selling you begin to lose confidence, reducing sales further; then you start worrying about your job, your future and how to pay bills – and the vicious circle continues.

The first step in eliminating worry is to recognise the futility of it. What did worry achieve for you in the past? Ulcers? Sleepless nights? Migraine attacks? Family feuds? Did all that worry contribute positively to your difficulty in the slightest manner? The answer is no!

When you worry, 85% of people don't care and the other 15% are delighted, according to one reformed worrier. Research carried out on people affected by worry indicated that:

50% of worries come from past events;
40% come from things that haven't happened yet;
10% apply to what is happening today.

If these figures are correct (and I believe they are) 90% of our troubles can be written off because we can do absolutely nothing about them. I realise that for some people this is easier said than done. However, worry is only a bad habit and habits can be changed.

Worries are invariably looked on as serious 'problems' and few people have been trained in how to cope with or handle them. One successful method of dealing with them is to convert them into 'situations'. By looking at a worry or difficulty as a 'situation' your mental perception changes from one of 'I can't handle this' to 'What can I do to alter this situation?' It does, of course, require a different kind of thinking but it really does work. Try it!

Another formula for eliminating worry is to write it all down on a sheet of paper and analyse all the options open to you. Take any problem or situation that is presently causing you concern and fill in the following:

1. What am I worrying about? _____

2. What are the facts? _____

3. What is the cause of the problem? _____

4. What can I do about it? What are the implications?

    Option 1

    Option 2

    Option 3

    Option 4

    Option 5

5. The best solution is _____

6. The worst that can possibly happen is _____

7. I will implement this solution (date) _____

Handling stress

Selling enters into every form of human activity. A top salesperson is a counsellor, a manager, a financial wizard, a mathematician, a judge, a product expert, a complaints manager, a telephone expert, a writer, a reader, a listener, a saint, a magician and a top communicator. In addition, he or she has to go out and sell. Inevitably this brings on stress and not everybody is capable of coping with it.

Like so many other things, stress can have two extremes, too much or too little, and it can be fatal or fantastic. Let us take too little stress: as an example, when a person retires and all the 'industrial stress' is removed, he or she just may not cope without the stress. On the other hand, if stress is bad for you, how come most people perform at their peak in situations of high-level stress, such as the Olympics and world championships?

Before the industrial revolution, men lived longer than women. The stress of paying mortgaes on time each month, overcrowding and a host of other social pressures have been responsible for reversing the position.

If we could all learn to cope with the stresses imposed by society we might live a little longer. The medical world claim the human body is built to last 100–150 years: if so, many of us are going to be grossly shortchanged.

Medical experts claim that people who have *too much* stress in their lives should learn to say 'no'. Why impose unnecessary pressures? Cease to be a passenger and become the driver. *You* decide what is good for you.

People who have *too little* stress should learn to say 'yes' and start taking a more active interest in their own lives.

Too much or too little stress obviously affects your health eventually. The Chinese have a good way of explaining the importance of it. They believe that when you declare each of your 'assets', such as happiness, wealth, status, position, ability and so on, you score 0. For health, your prime asset, you score 1. If you were in top physical condition and you perceived health to be your best asset you would have the 1 followed by all the 0s – like so: 1,000,000. In other words, your assets' value is determined by where you place health in the order of priorities. Take the opposite example – where you judge your health to be your least asset – and the figure now looks like this: 000,000,1. You can see immediately how useful your other assets are.

Many things contribute to bad health: we are told every day to 'stop smoking', 'get more exercise', 'eat properly'. Many of us ignore these admonitions until it is too late. Our western diet deficiencies are a major debilitating factor. In conversation a food allergist told me that after the Korean War, autopsies were carried out on 300 GIs and 300 Korean soldiers. While it is little consolation, the 300 Koreans died in good health, whereas the Americans had many medical disorders; the cause – western diet.

On my courses, when the subject of stress arises, we find health comes into the discussion, and this brings us on to the topic of different types of medicine. I know many people who have benefited from this information, so I shall pass on a personal experience. First a little background.

After three years of treatment by conventional medicine for a mysterious stomach upset I experienced no improvement. While the complaint never stopped me working, it was uncomfortable when I got the attacks. It was suggested I should see an allergist or a doctor practising homoeopathic medicine. Very sceptical, but with nothing to lose, I went to see an allergist and discovered to my surprise that I was allergic to caffeine. Once I started on decaffeinated coffee the discomfort disappeared. I became intensely interested in alternative medicine and discovered some important information that others have found helpful.

If you have some ailment that conventional medicine has failed to relieve or cure, check out the alternatives. It may be that the acne, pains in the back or stomach, or rashes on the exposed parts of the body are a reaction to unsuitable diet. Just because you have never had the problem before does not necessarily mean that you haven't developed it. A sales girl who had suffered from acne for 12 years had been treated with a special type of cortisone cream with no effect. The allergist discovered she was allergic to yeast (in white bread) and sugar. She eliminated these elements from her diet and for the first time in 12 years she had clear skin.

I have nothing but the highest regard for conventional medicine but there are times when alternatives should be considered in specific cases. If you are interested in pursuing this subject you may consider reading the following books:

The Joy of Stress by Dr Peter Hansen (Pan Books);
Allergies: What Everyone Should Know by Keith Mumby, MB, ChB (Unwin Paperbacks).

One of the first steps to reducing stress or improving health is to be aware of the factors that are causing it in the first place. The second stage is to decide what you are going to do about it. The final and most important is the benefits to you of carrying out your chosen action:

Causes of stress in my life:	What I can do:	Benefits to me will be:

The importance of being different

Most of us work in competitive markets and the more competitive the market the more opportunity there is to be different. Our objective is to be perceived by our customers as the most professional salesperson with whom to deal.

Talk to customers who buy in highly competitive markets and they will confirm that buying is no longer an easy task. The following quote from a buyer sums up the difficulties in making a purchase:

'Today, more than at any time previously, with so many companies so active in the same market, making a decision to buy can be a draining experience. Theoretically, if I wanted to meet with every salesperson marketing copiers in this area I would have to talk to about 60 different people. If I want a fax machine, a telephone system, printing, stationery, or just about anything for the office, I will have a similar number of companies to choose from. I can't talk to all of

163

them and the more people I talk to the more confusing it will become. With so little to separate one company from the other it may well be down to the salespeople to prove to me that they can offer something that the others cannot.'

How one can be different is a matter for the individual. To achieve and claim uniqueness it is imperative to know the strengths and weaknesses of your rivals:

- What can you offer that they cannot? If it is unique, make sure that every customer knows about it.
- What are *they* doing that you are not? How can you do it better?
- Ask your customers what they expect from you and your company and give it to them. (Just asking the question may make you unique.)
- Do you make a habit of remembering and using the names of the buyer's colleagues and staff?
- Do you write personal letters to customers thanking them for the orders and assuring them of having made a good decision?
- Do you write to customers who do not make a purchase and thank them for their time?
- When customers send in a cheque do you ensure they are phoned and thanked? Many companies will pay any amount of money to remind the customer that they haven't.

In order to be different, one must acquire a creative imagination. On my courses I show a badly designed wheelbarrow and ask the delegates to write down their *comments*. Not surprisingly, an invitation to *comment* is usually perceived as an opportunity to point out the things that are 'wrong'. Practically all comments turn out to be criticisms, such as: 'the handle is too short'; 'the wheel is in the wrong place'; and 'the design is impractical for proper use'. It is remarkable that only one in a thousand will see the many positive aspects. If you show the same design to 10-year-old children, they will invariably see only the positive characteristics.

The question is, are you a 'creative' person? *Narrow-minded* people see only *one* point of view – their own; *reasonable* people see *both* sides of every debatable subject; *creative* people see *three* sides:

1. the negative side;

2. the positive side;

3. the interesting aspects.

A creative approach gives salespeople the competitive edge because they lead with positive and stimulating ideas and allow their rivals to flounder in mediocrity.

The creative salesperson is:

- open to the views and ideas of others;
- hungry for knowledge;
- not discouraged by failure;
- prepared to persevere in the face of opposition.

Creative salespeople believe that:

- every problem creates an opportunity;
- to every problem there is a solution;
- making mistakes is a learning experience;
- ideas are multiplied by seeking the ideas of others.

Creative salespeople keep asking:

- Why am I doing it this way?
- How long shall I be doing it this way?
- Is there a better way?
- Have we tried any other way?

Go in to win the order every time

At any competitive event, such as the Olympic Games, it often requires sophisticated equipment to separate the winner from the second-placed athlete. What it confirms is that the winner gave that little 'extra'. The second athlete has some consolation in taking the silver medal. In selling terms we can draw some comparisons. Many times a sale is won by the salesperson who contributes extra effort, but unlike the sporting world there are no prizes for coming second.

Selling is a race where only the first past the post scoops the prize.

Some years ago Martina Navratilova was asked what inspired her to such heights of success as a tennis player. She replied that she made a decision early in her career that she wanted to be the very best. She always knew it would be easy to be mediocre but, if she was going to be the best, it was really going to hurt.

Selling is no different from any other occupation. If you are not approaching customers with the sincere intention of getting the order, you are a square peg in a round hole.

Be positive

Throughout my sales career I have had the great privilege of being associated with several thousand salespeople. They were made up of colleagues, my own salespeople, delegates on development programmes and rivals. The rest were people I had the opportunity to see in action in different parts of Europe and the United States. A question once asked by a delegate at a seminar inspired a considered analysis as to why some salespeople are successful while others are not. I thought about this at great length and came to the following conclusions:

- The distinguishing characteristic of all people who achieve success is their attitude. I have yet to meet anybody who was consistently successful at anything with a bad attitude. Socially, it was a pleasure to be in the company of these successful people. They were stimulating personalities and enjoyable conversationalists. The combination of talent and style, refined on the anvil of experience, inspired customer confidence.
- They had a messianic belief in the company that employed them and had supreme faith in the quality of their products and the viability of the services proferred.

Success can be achieved only by positive thoughts whereas every negative thought has a negative result. These positive thoughts must be accompanied by a sincere desire to succeed because it is desire, not ability, that is the more powerful factor.

Why is it that some people seem to achieve tremendous success, recognition and personal satisfaction with little apparent effort? Why do others achieve their goals only with tremendous effort and sacrifice, while others, equally hardworking, never seem to achieve anything worthwhile at all? Why should there be such a disparity in the levels of success? It is self-evident that it is not something that is hereditary, and it is not physical; so it must come from within.

I do not believe that ability plays such a big part in the success or failure of salespeople. The most successful that I have known were of average ability and intelligence. I have also met, and so have you, many people with enormous talent who succeed at nothing. The reason is simple – they lack the desire to succeed.

Andrew Carnegie, the great American industrialist, once said: 'Give me a man of average ability, but with a burning desire to succeed, and I will show you a winner in return, every time.'

Take the situation of salesperson A who struggles through her sales target month after month. The company introduce an attractive sales incentive for improved sales importance and this lady not only achieves her new target but breaks sales records on the way. It happens in practically every sales organisation every day. Do these people suddenly change their ability? Of course not. What has changed is the desire and motivation to succeed.

Maintaining a positive attitude can be quite difficult, but less so when one is conscious of the other hidden pressures to fail, such as psychological 'ceilings' imposed by others. In this regard I have a personal experience to relate.

Having worked for an international company for five years, I was offered a position with a new and successful organisation. My induction training in London wasn't to take place for six days. The sales manager suggested that I should familiarise myself with the territory and product. 'If you pick up a sale here and there all the better.' I worked my territory for six days and opened 14 accounts. The sales manager said nothing about my first week's performance, so I headed off to London, anxious to get my induction training over with and return to my territory.

This company employed over 2,000 sales personnel and every week they received the in-company sales bulletin with the top sales performance highlighted, with a few complimentary comments from the sales director. Not being aware of the existence of this bulletin, I was stunned when senior executives and salespeople kept congratulating me on a 'fantasic achievement' and a 'superlative performance', and making other complimentary remarks. 'How did you open 14 accounts in one week, when most of us have difficulty in opening one?' was a typical question. Because they had made such a big deal about it I began to question myself about my 'freak' performance. I was reminded constantly that the company target was eight accounts per month and most salespeople had great difficulty achieving it.

For the remainder of my time with that company I was never to achieve anything even remotely resembling that 'freak' performance. In fact, I struggled to achieve in one month what I had previously achieved in one week – my first. I had allowed other people to convince me that there was a 'ceiling' in selling and my first week's performance was 'abnormal'.

Those who succeed are those who really believe they will.

It was some years before I realised that, through the comments of others, I had imposed psychological ceilings on my own ability to sell.

To what limitations are you working? Is it possible for you to achieve a higher turnover than what is asked for? Have you allowed yourself to be conditioned by the performance of your predecessors? If your life depended on doubling your sales, could you do it?

Here is an appraisal form (an extra form is included at the end of the book). By using your own judgement, rate your score on how you see yourself now. The other forms should be completed periodically over the next few weeks. If you digest all the suggestions and complete all the action steps you will notice a big improvement in your sales performance, attitude and confidence.

Selling skills performance appraisal

Score	0	1	2	3	4	5	6	7	8	9	10
Appearance and manner											
Planning and administration											
Attitude to colleagues & managers											
Attitude to company & policy											
Attitude to customers & problems											
Attitude to product											
Time management											
Territory management											
Decision-making ability											
Use of imagination											
Product knowledge											
Competitor knowledge											
Customer knowledge											
Ability to get new business											
Telephone technique											
Initial impression on customer											
Opening statements											
Establishing rapport											
Buying motives identified											
Conversation balance											
Making the presentation											
Handling objections											
Closing the sale											
Parting impression											
After-sales service											
Post-call analysis											
Relevance of material											
Condition of sales material											

◀ BIBLIOGRAPHY ▶

Adair, John (1981) *Training for Communication*, Gower Publishing Co Ltd, Aldershot.

Allen, Robert Y, Spohn, Robert F and Wilson, I Herbert (1984) *Selling Dynamics*, McGraw Hill, New York, USA.

Anderson, B Robert (1981) *Professional Selling*, Second Edition, Prentice-Hall, New Jersey, USA.

Bettger, Frank (1977) *How I Multiplied My Income and Happiness in Selling*, Cedar Book, Windmill Press, Tadworth.

Bliss, Edwin C *Getting Things Done. The ABCs of Time Management*, Bantam Books, Inc, New York, USA.

Campbell, David (1977) *Take The Road to Creativity and Get Off Your Dead End*, Argus Communications, Illinois, USA.

Carnegie, Dale (1981) *How To Win Friends and Influence People*, Pocket Books, New York, USA.

Dellinger, Susan and Deane, Barbara (1980) *Communicating Effectively. A Complete Guide for Better Managing*, Chilton Book Company, Pennsylvania, USA.

Fensterheim, Herbert and Baer, Jean (1980) *Don't Say Yes When You Want To Say No. The Assertiveness Training Book*, Dell Publishing Co Inc, New York, USA.

Fenton, John (1981) *The A-Z of Sales Management*, Pan Business Sales, London.

Fenton, John (1986) *How To Sell Against Competition*, Pan Business Management, London.

Goldmann, Heinz M (1980) *How To Win Customers. The Classic Manual of Successful Selling*, Revised Edition, Pan Business Sales, London.

Hanson, Peter (1987) *The Joy of Stress*, Pan Books Ltd, London.

Harris, Thomas A (1973) *I'm OK – You're OK. Climb out of the cellar of your mind....* Pan Books Ltd, London.

Hill, Napoleon (1966) *Think and Grow Rich*, Melvin Powers, Wilshire Book Company, California, USA.

Hill, Napoleon and Stone, W Clement (1977) *Success Through a Positive Mental Attitude*, Pocket Books, New York, USA.

Knaus, William J (1979) *Do It Now. How to Stop Procrastinating*, Prentice-Hall Inc, New Jersey, USA.

Koerper, Philip J (1980) *How To Talk Your Way to Success in Selling*, Reward Books, New York USA.

LeBoeuf, Michael (1979) *Working Smart. How to Accomplish More in Half the Time*, Warner Books in arrangement with McGraw-Hill, New York USA.

Lorayne, Harry and Lucas, Jerry (1980) *The Memory Book*, Ballantine Books, New York, USA.

Mercer, David (1988) *The Sales Professional. Strategies and Techniques for Managing the High-Level Sale*, Kogan Page, London.

Mills, Kenneth H and Paul, Judith E (1979) *Successful Retail Sales.* Prentice-Hall Inc, New Jersey, USA.

Morris, Desmond (1986) *The Pocket Guide to Manwatching*, Triad Grafton Books, London.

Nordstrom, Richard D (1981) *Introduction to Selling. An Experimental Approach to Skill Development.* Macmillan Publishing Co Inc, New York/Collier Macmillan Publishers, London.

Oldcorn, Roger (1982) *Management*, Pan Breakthrough Books, London.

Pease, Allan (1984) *Signals. How To Use Body Language For Power, Success and Love*, Bantam Books, New York, USA.

Peel, Malcolm (1987) *Customer Service. How to Achieve Total Customer Satisfaction*, Kogan Page, London.

Silva, José (1983) *The Silva Mind Control Method*, Granada Publishing, London.

Stanton, Nicki (1981) *The Business of Communicating. Improving Your Communication Skills*, Pan Breakthrough Books, London.

Stanton, Nicki (1982) *What Do You Mean 'Communication'? An Introduction to Communication in Business.* Pan Breakthrough Books, London.

Tack, Alfred (1987) *1000 Ways To Increase Your Sales*, Cedar Books, London.

◀ INDEX ▶

Selling skills performance appraisal

Score	0	1	2	3	4	5	6	7	8	9	10
Appearance and manner											
Planning and administration											
Attitude to colleagues & managers											
Attitude to company & policy											
Attitude to customers & problems											
Attitude to product											
Time management											
Territory management											
Decision-making ability											
Use of imagination											
Product knowledge											
Competitor knowledge											
Customer knowledge											
Ability to get new business											
Telephone technique											
Initial impression on customer											
Opening statements											
Establishing rapport											
Buying motives identified											
Conversation balance											
Making the presentation											
Handling objections											
Closing the sale											
Parting impression											
After-sales service											
Post-call analysis											
Relevance of material											
Condition of sales material											